Frontiers in Civil Engineering
(Volume 5)

Systematic Architectural Design for Optimal Wind Energy Generation

Authored by

Abdel Rahman Elbakheit
College of Architecture and Planning
Department of Architecture and Building Sciences
King Saud University
Riyadh
Saudi Arabia

Frontiers in Civil Engineering

Volume # 5

Systematic Architectural Design for Optimal Wind Energy Generation

Author: Abdel Rahman Elbakheit

ISSN (Online): 2468-4708

ISSN (Print): 2468-4694

ISBN (Online): 978-1-68108-850-1

ISBN (Print): 978-1-68108-851-8

ISBN (Paperback): 978-1-68108-852-5

© 2021, Bentham Books imprint.

Published by Bentham Science Publishers – Sharjah, UAE. All Rights Reserved.

BENTHAM SCIENCE PUBLISHERS LTD.
End User License Agreement (for non-institutional, personal use)

This is an agreement between you and Bentham Science Publishers Ltd. Please read this License Agreement carefully before using the ebook/echapter/ejournal (**"Work"**). Your use of the Work constitutes your agreement to the terms and conditions set forth in this License Agreement. If you do not agree to these terms and conditions then you should not use the Work.

Bentham Science Publishers agrees to grant you a non-exclusive, non-transferable limited license to use the Work subject to and in accordance with the following terms and conditions. This License Agreement is for non-library, personal use only. For a library / institutional / multi user license in respect of the Work, please contact: permission@benthamscience.net.

Usage Rules:

1. All rights reserved: The Work is 1. the subject of copyright and Bentham Science Publishers either owns the Work (and the copyright in it) or is licensed to distribute the Work. You shall not copy, reproduce, modify, remove, delete, augment, add to, publish, transmit, sell, resell, create derivative works from, or in any way exploit the Work or make the Work available for others to do any of the same, in any form or by any means, in whole or in part, in each case without the prior written permission of Bentham Science Publishers, unless stated otherwise in this License Agreement.
2. You may download a copy of the Work on one occasion to one personal computer (including tablet, laptop, desktop, or other such devices). You may make one back-up copy of the Work to avoid losing it.
3. The unauthorised use or distribution of copyrighted or other proprietary content is illegal and could subject you to liability for substantial money damages. You will be liable for any damage resulting from your misuse of the Work or any violation of this License Agreement, including any infringement by you of copyrights or proprietary rights.

Disclaimer:

Bentham Science Publishers does not guarantee that the information in the Work is error-free, or warrant that it will meet your requirements or that access to the Work will be uninterrupted or error-free. The Work is provided "as is" without warranty of any kind, either express or implied or statutory, including, without limitation, implied warranties of merchantability and fitness for a particular purpose. The entire risk as to the results and performance of the Work is assumed by you. No responsibility is assumed by Bentham Science Publishers, its staff, editors and/or authors for any injury and/or damage to persons or property as a matter of products liability, negligence or otherwise, or from any use or operation of any methods, products instruction, advertisements or ideas contained in the Work.

Limitation of Liability:

In no event will Bentham Science Publishers, its staff, editors and/or authors, be liable for any damages, including, without limitation, special, incidental and/or consequential damages and/or damages for lost data and/or profits arising out of (whether directly or indirectly) the use or inability to use the Work. The entire liability of Bentham Science Publishers shall be limited to the amount actually paid by you for the Work.

General:

1. Any dispute or claim arising out of or in connection with this License Agreement or the Work (including non-contractual disputes or claims) will be governed by and construed in accordance with the laws of the U.A.E. as applied in the Emirate of Dubai. Each party agrees that the courts of the Emirate of Dubai shall have exclusive jurisdiction to settle any dispute or claim arising out of or in connection with this License Agreement or the Work (including non-contractual disputes or claims).
2. Your rights under this License Agreement will automatically terminate without notice and without the

need for a court order if at any point you breach any terms of this License Agreement. In no event will any delay or failure by Bentham Science Publishers in enforcing your compliance with this License Agreement constitute a waiver of any of its rights.
3. You acknowledge that you have read this License Agreement, and agree to be bound by its terms and conditions. To the extent that any other terms and conditions presented on any website of Bentham Science Publishers conflict with, or are inconsistent with, the terms and conditions set out in this License Agreement, you acknowledge that the terms and conditions set out in this License Agreement shall prevail.

Bentham Science Publishers Ltd.
Executive Suite Y - 2
PO Box 7917, Saif Zone
Sharjah, U.A.E.
Email: subscriptions@benthamscience.net

CONTENTS

PREFACE	i
CONSENT FOR PUBLICATION	ii
CONFLICT OF INTEREST	ii
ACKNOWLEDGEMENTS	ii
REFERENCES	ii
CHAPTER 1 WIND AND ARCHITECTURE	1
1. INTRODUCTION	1
2. EXAMPLES OF FULLY DEVELOPED ARCHITECTURAL DESIGNS FOR WIND ENERGY HARVESTING	3
2.1. Bahrain World Trade Center	3
2.2. Strata SE1	5
2.3. Pearl River Tower	7
3. WIND AND ARCHITECTURAL SAFETY	10
3.1. Wind-induced Vibration in Buildings—Definition and Cause	10
3.2. Wind-induced Vibration in Buildings—Remedies and Measures	11
3.3. Performance Criteria for Tall Buildings under Wind Design	13
3.3.1. Human Comfort	13
4. BUILDING'S AERODYNAMIC PERFORMANCE	13
CONCLUSION	21
REFERENCES	22
CHAPTER 2 AERODYNAMIC ARCHITECTURAL DESIGN	24
1. INTRODUCTION	24
2. REASONS FOR AERODYNAMIC ARCHITECTURAL DESIGN	25
2.1. Ventilation	25
2.1.1. Natural Wind Pressure	25
2.1.2. Displacement or Stack Ventilation	26
2.1.3. Bernoulli Effect	27
2.1.4. Venturi Tube	27
2.1.5. Types of Wind Flows: Laminar, Separated, Turbulent or Eddy Flows	28
2.1.6. Air Inertia	30
2.1.7. No Vacuum in the Atmosphere	31
3. WIND ENERGY HARVESTING	31
3.1. Building Design Optimisation for Potential Wind Energy Collection	31
3.1.1. Overview	31
3.2. Aerodynamic Aerofoils for Wind Energy Generation	34
CONCLUSION	37
REFERENCES	37
CHAPTER 3 WIND AS AN ON-SITE ENERGY SOURCE	39
1. INTRODUCTION	39
2. WIND ENERGY AVAILABILITY	40
3. WIND AVAILABILITY WITH HEIGHT	43
4. VARIABILITY	48
5. CAPACITY FACTOR	49
CONCLUSION	49
REFERENCES	49
CHAPTER 4 ARCHITECTURAL AEROFOIL FORM OPTIMISATION FOR WIND ENERGY GENERATION	51

1. INTRODUCTION 51
2. ANALYSIS OF WIND TURBINE INTEGRATION INTO BUILDING DESIGN 52
   2.1. Assumptions 52
   2.2. Wind Turbine Integration 53
   2.3. Optimising Aerofoil Proximity to Roof Surface 54
   2.4. Underlying Simulation Strategies 54
   2.5. Computational Fluid Dynamics 56
      2.5.1. Effect of Domain Size 57
      2.5.1. Mesh-independent Solution 57
      2.5.3. Grid Convergence Study 58
   2.6. The Effect of Models of Turbulence 59
   2.7. The Effect of the Aerofoil Position on Top of the Roof 62
   2.8. The Effect of Different Wind Directions 64
   2.9. Summary of Optimising the Aerofoil Proximity to the Roof of the House 65
   2.10. Summary of Optimisation of the Aerofoil Front Shape 66
   2.11. Effect of Increasing the Angle of Attack 67
3. POWER ESTIMATION 68
   3.1. Effect of Aerofoil Angle of Attack and Aerofoil Proximity on the Power Output 69
CONCLUSION 70
REFERENCES 71

CHAPTER 5 BUILDING-INTEGRATED WIND TURBINES 73
1. INTRODUCTION 73
2. NOISE REDUCTION OR PREVENTION 74
3. WIND-INDUCED VIBRATIONS IN WIND TURBINES 75
4. INCREASING WIND VELOCITY FOR WIND TURBINES 76
   4.1. Diffuser Design Evolution 76
   4.2. Technical Background 77
   4.3. Velocity and Pressure of the Diffuser 79
   4.4. Classifications of Ducted Wind Turbines 80
      4.4.1. Simple Diffusers 81
      4.4.2. Multi-slot Diffuser 82
      4.4.3. Brim or Flange Diffuser 82
      4.4.4. Vorticity-based Diffuser/Turbine 83
      4.4.5. Mixer Ejector Wind Turbine 84
      4.4.6. Rotating Diffuser 85
CONCLUSION 86
REFERENCES 86

CHAPTER 6 EFFECT OF TURBINE RESISTANCE AND POSITIONING ON THE PERFORMANCE OF AEROFOIL BUILDING-AUGMENTED WIND ENERGY GENERATION 88
1. INTRODUCTION 88
2. EFFECT OF TURBINE RESISTANCE ON RESULTING VELOCITIES AND FLOW PATTERNS 89
   2.1. Effect of Turbine Resistance on Wind Flow Patterns 90
   2.2. Effect of Turbine Resistance on Resulting Wind Velocities 92
3. EFFECT OF TURBINE RESISTANCE ON RESULTING PRESSURE COEFFICIENT 94
4. EFFECT OF TURBINE RESISTANCE ON RESULTING POWER GENERATION 96
5. TURBINE POSITIONS UNDER THE AEROFOIL 99
6. EFFECT OF BUILDING HEIGHT ON RESULTING WIND VELOCITIES 100
   6.1. Results of the Effect of Building Height 102

CONCLUSION	103
REFERENCES	104
CHAPTER 7 CONCLUSION	**105**
SUBJECT INDEX	109

PREFACE

With a better understanding of building sciences and improved technologies for the utilisation of building physics, architectural form-finding processes became more elaborated with the added consideration for thermal, acoustic, solar, and aerodynamic forms. Majority of these invisible ordering principles have been developed in the last 100 years; however, they have impacted critical decisions about architectural form only in about the last 70 years. The science of architectural acoustics, for example, did not exist until the second half of the twentieth century, and practical auditorium acoustics were not well understood until about 1960s.

The advent and evolution of building sciences and their incorporation into building technologies transformed the means of evaluating architecture. Thus, several qualitative aspects of architectural form were measurable in quantitative terms. Other than all the general means of spatial experience, comfort, music, lighting, colour, and energy requirements could also be measured, totally optimised and reconfigured.

This book concentrates on further elaborations on the influences of wind and architecture on building sciences, architectural form finding and the optimisation of wind energy harvesting using suitable wind turbines. This publication documents case studies on existing buildings' designs incorporating wind energy technology in Chapter 1. Certain processes and key indicators for evaluating and testing any envisioned architectural form have been proposed in this chapter. Moreover, the methods for scanning various wind aerodynamic responses relevant to buildings that could be utilised for wind energy harvesting have been elaborated, along with the various types of wind flows and their characteristics. Further steps for streamlining architectural forms to generate optimal wind flows prior to energy harvesting are discussed in Chapter 2.

The ideas presented in this book are a continuation to previous work, aiming to enhance architectural design potential for achieving better prospects of sustainability through the assimilation of wind energy harvesting into architectural form design. In Chapters 4 and 6, the works presented in publications titled, 'Factors enhancing aerofoil wings for wind energy harnessing in buildings'[1] and 'Effect of turbine resistance and positioning on performance of Aerofoil wing building augmented wind energy generation' [2], respectively, are further elaborated. The former study examines how architectural form and aerofoils together can be manipulated to generate continuous wind flows suitable for energy harvesting using wind turbines. Some aerofoil forms are proposed on the basis of their aerodynamic qualities and peculiar attributes capable of assisting wind flow patterns around buildings. The latter study examines different positions of turbines within the same design aspects envisioned in the former study on wind energy harvesting. An independent tool is needed to be employed to 'measure' these attributes of design, which was done in the form of fluid flow computations using computational fluid dynamics (CFD).

Although the content of this study has a well-established scientific basis to it, together with this tool, the design decisions are still on pure architectural forms and their merits of clean energy generation and maximisation. This reflects the capability of a design to transcend the boundaries of science and art in a more unifying and encompassing way. One would recall the following from Richard Buchanan's 'Wicked Problems in Design Thinking', in Margolin and Buchanan, eds., The Idea of Design, 1995:

'The significance of seeking a scientific basis for design does not lie in the likelihood of reducing design to one or another of the sciences. . . . Rather, it lies in a concern to connect and integrate useful knowledge from the arts and sciences alike'.

In Chapter 5, a thorough review of diffuser augmentation technology for wind turbines amenable to building integration and/or mimicking in architectural forms is undertaken. The key dimensional proportions of a diffuser that critically underlie augmentation level/success and in turn that is suitable for inclusion within an architectural form are highlighted.

In Chapter 7, the overall conclusions and suggestions are elaborated. In case of any feedback, please contact the author at the following email address: abdel.elbakheit@hotmail.com

CONSENT FOR PUBLICATION

Not applicable.

CONFLICT OF INTEREST

The author declares no conflict of interest, financial or otherwise.

ACKNOWLEDGEMENTS

Declared none.

REFERENCES

[1] Elbakheit A.R., "Factors enhancing aerofoil wings for wind energy harnessing in buildings", *Build. Serv. Eng. Res. Tech,* vol. 35, no. 4, pp. 417-437, 2014.
[http://dx.doi.org/10.1177/0143624413509097]

[2] Elbakheit A.R., "Effect of turbine resistance and positioning on performance of Aerofoil wing building augmented wind energy generation", *Energy and Buildings,* vol. 174, pp. 365-371, 2018.
[http://dx.doi.org/10.1016/j.enbuild.2018.06.025]

Abdel Rahman Elbakheit
College of Architecture and Planning
Department of Architecture and Building Sciences
King Saud University
Riyadh
Saudi Arabia
Email: abdel.elbakheit@hotmail.com

CHAPTER 1

Wind and Architecture

Abstract: In this chapter, the influences of wind on architecture are highlighted. Wind can have both positive and negative effects on architecture. Moreover, architecture can respond in proactive ways to maximise the benefits of wind forces and reduce or eliminate the negative impacts. This chapter sheds further light on notable architectural ideas translated into architectural case studies on harvesting wind energy in the built environment. Moreover, this chapter enables gaining insight into successful practices in architectural design solutions and ways and means to further enhance the performance of the buildings. In addition, the negative impacts of high wind velocities are identified, and possible solutions to mitigate them at their source are presented and discussed. Optimised architectural forms that can completely avoid excessive wind forces and devastating vortex shedding during the design stage are presented.

Keywords: Architectural forms, Aerodynamic architectural optimisation, Architectural form finding, Architectural stability, Vortex shedding, Wind energy, Wind energy harvesting, Wind forces.

1. INTRODUCTION

Mankind encountered wind and its effects from the dawn of existence. The history of using this renewable energy source has been well integrated in human civilisation, being implemented for sailing boats and operating wind mills [1], wind catchers [2], *etc*. However, for buildings in general, architectural form in particular, wind is associated either with structural safety or ventilation of interior spaces. With technology advancement, structural safety and ventilation have developed to be well established aspects of architectural form, although under different specialisations: structural safety under structural engineering [3] and ventilation under mechanical engineering [4]. However, architectural design retained the initiative of combining these two, among others, to produce more environmentally friendly buildings. Thus, the need to adequately benefit from wind arose. In other words, the need to find a way to tame the giant to harvest its energy at the point where it is made. In this regard, some notable conceptual architectural ideas put forth by architect Bill Dunster [5] were ground breaking, wherein he proposed the integration of a flower-shaped structure with at Tall building concentrating and accelerating wind flow for energy harvesting. Another wind energy harvesting design was developed by the European funded project of 'WEB – JOR3-CT98-0270' [September 1998–August 2000] [6], which performed a systematic study on the generation of wind flows by design manipulation to enhance wind energy harvesting. This study included the use of two large kidney-shaped towers that channel and accelerate wind flows between them, where large turbines are present. A prototype was erected and tested. Fig. (**1**) shows this prototype, which was designed under the collaborative efforts of Imperial College London, Mecal applied mechanics (*i.e.*, consulting firm), University of Stuttgart, and BDSP partnership Ltd. (*i.e.*, engineering consulting firm). This project highlighted that this architectural design enabled increasing wind energy generation by a factor of at least 25% compared with the annual yield of the same turbines under a standalone scenario.

Fig. (1). Conceptual architectural design of kidney-shaped twin towers with three horizontal-axis wind turbines integrated, having diameters of 35 m and generating 250 kW of power [8].

Derek Tayler of Altechnica [7] invented 'the Aeolian roof' that contained a pitched roof with a flat wing at the ridge, which accelerated wind in this area. Wind turbines were then proposed to be used to harvest energy from this accelerated wind.

In 2005, a report was published from the joint venture of the Carbon Trust UK and some consulting and research bodies such as Imperial College London and Altechnica. It detailed the potential of building-integrated wind turbines.

2. EXAMPLES OF FULLY DEVELOPED ARCHITECTURAL DESIGNS FOR WIND ENERGY HARVESTING

Recently, some projects involving architectural forms incorporating wind turbines have been completed around the globe, such as the Bahrain World Trade Center (BWTC) in Manama, Bahrain, Strata SE1 in London, UK, and Pearl River Tower in Guangzhou, China.

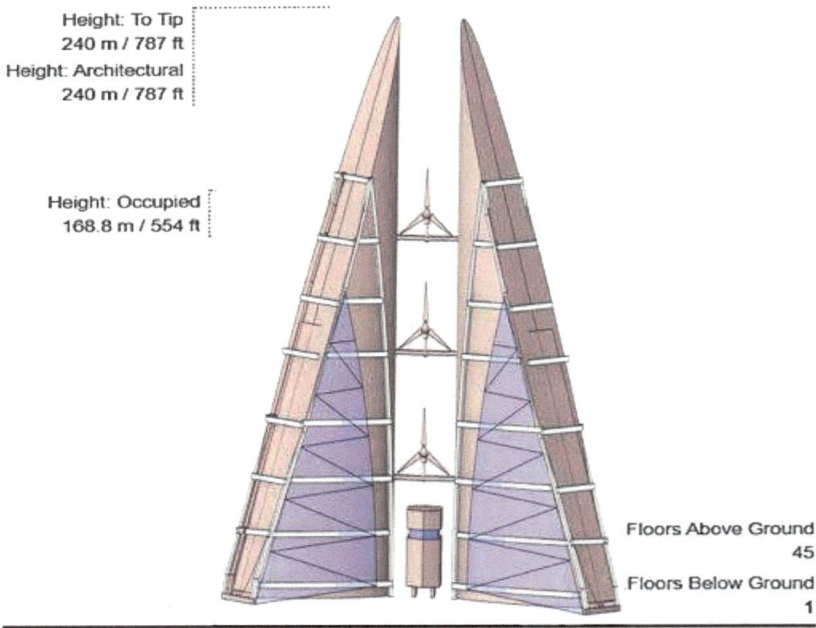

Fig. (2). Schematic of the Bahrain World Trade Center, Gulf view.

2.1. Bahrain World Trade Center

The BWTC is a manifestation of architectural form finding with wind energy integration (Figs. 2 and 3). The BWTC [9] cleverly integrates the natural wind flow patterns of the wind exchange between the Arabian Gulf and land shore in what is scientifically known as the 'sea–land breeze' phenomenon. The BWTC's main axis is parallel to the gulf coast; thus, it faces the natural wind passage from land and sea at all times.

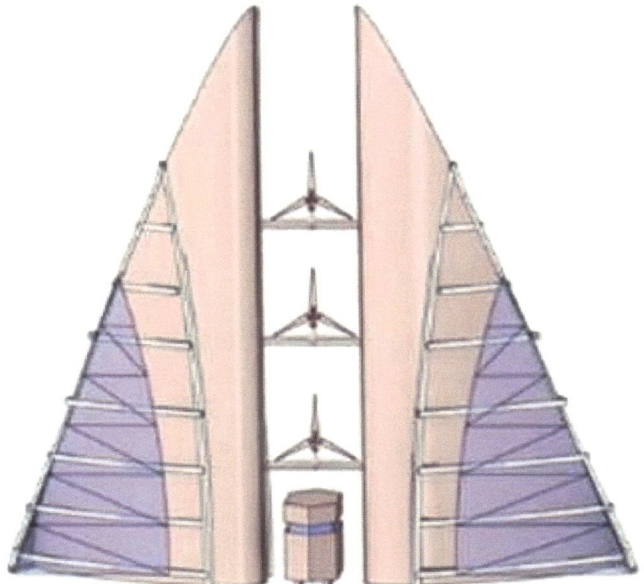

Fig. (3). Schematic of the Bahrain World Trade Centre, land view.

The elliptical form of the BWTC layout assists the wind flow in finding its way between the twin towers, further accelerating the flow.

As the twin towers taper skywards, the three-dimensional (3D) aerofoil sections gradually reduce in size, thus providing more stability to the architectural form and securing it from vortex shedding, which is discussed further in section 3.1. This effect (*i.e.*, stability from vertex shedding) reinforced with the accelerating onshore wind velocity between the towers and upwards, produces a pattern of wind velocity that is harvested by the three wind turbines.

The three turbines weigh 11 tons each, have a 29-m-diameter rotor and are supported on a 70-tons 31.5-m length bridge each. Annually, each turbine generates about 225 kW of power.

However sound, logical and well-grounded the scientific bases of these ideas may appear to be, this design necessitated large initial investments, and in the long run, maintenance could be an issue. In addition, there are other disadvantages such as loud noise and heavy vibrations. Furthermore, from the comments of the observers at the BWTC site, these turbines very rarely rotate. The actual reason for this is unclear. It could be either due to inadequate operations management or due to the wind velocities being much lower than anticipated. No comprehensive study on these turbines energy outcome is present at this moment.

2.2. Strata SE1

Strata SE1 [10] in London is another architectural design approach employing wind energy (Figs. **4** and **5**). The building houses about 408 residential flats. The architectural form is sculpted to provide maximum exposure to the south–southwest wind, which is the most prevailing wind direction, with the main façade facing this direction further enclaved (*i.e.*, curved) in a form of a sail to capture more wind. The leeward side has a triangular shape plan to further assist the main façade against the wind force. Wind is deflected upwards, accelerating it as it passes through the circular openings at the top of the building, where three wind turbines are placed, as shown in Figs. (**4** and **5**).

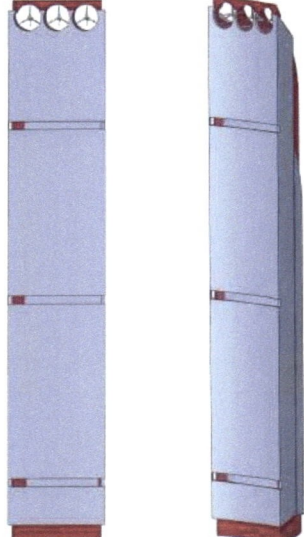

Fig. (4). Schematic of the main façade facing the prevailing wind direction of the Strata SE1.

Fig. (**4**) shows the schematic views of Strata SE1's main façade facing the prevailing wind direction. The turbine's energy feeds the common areas of the tower and the other landlord-controlled areas.

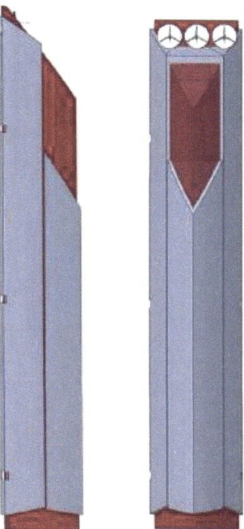

Fig. (5). Schematic of the façade of the leeward side of the Strata SE1.

Strata SE1 has 3-circular openings (Figs. **4** and **5**) each with a diameter of 9 m and contains three five-bladed turbines, each turbine producing 19 kW of power, which totals to about 50 MWh annual energy generation. This constitutes nearly 8% of the building's totally energy demand, which is approximately the consumption of 30 two-bedroom apartments, which are designed to 2006 UK's building regulations.

As for the BWTC, there is no sufficient follow-up study evaluating the turbines' performance or energy production for Strata SE1 in the literature.

Although these design ideas can be considered innovative, in practical terms, there are many limitations as to the need for the huge investments required to construct multiple towers as in the case of the BWTC, unless there are sound developmental, social or economic returns. Otherwise, additional solutions are required in terms of safety, which possibly result from the high wind velocities, noise, *etc*. However, when integrating wind energy harvesting systems with architecture, small-scale technologies that are capable of harvesting wind by utilising the wind flow around buildings, shortfalls of large plants or turbines can be avoided. The shortfalls of large plants have been the major obstacles faced during the proliferation of such projects due to their negative environmental impacts, such as noise and interference with natural light and artificial transmission of TV and radio broadcasting [11]. Moreover, the capital costs and the additional maintenance costs of the sophisticated machinery makes these designs less favourable. In contrast, *via* a small-scale and localised integration of wind energy harvesting technologies that need virtually no maintenance (*i.e.* no gear box as it runs on low speeds), such as incorporating wind turbines into existing or new buildings, more efficient utilisation of the available wind/ buildings resources could be achieved. Thus, the need for huge investments for incorporating large turbines within tall buildings or wind farms could be reduced.

2.3. Pearl River Tower

Pearl River Tower is a perfect example of an architectural design that is optimised for form and performance with considerable harmony in terms of the green or net zero energy principles [12] (Figs. **6 - 9**). The architectural form is carefully designed to enable harvesting both wind and solar energy.

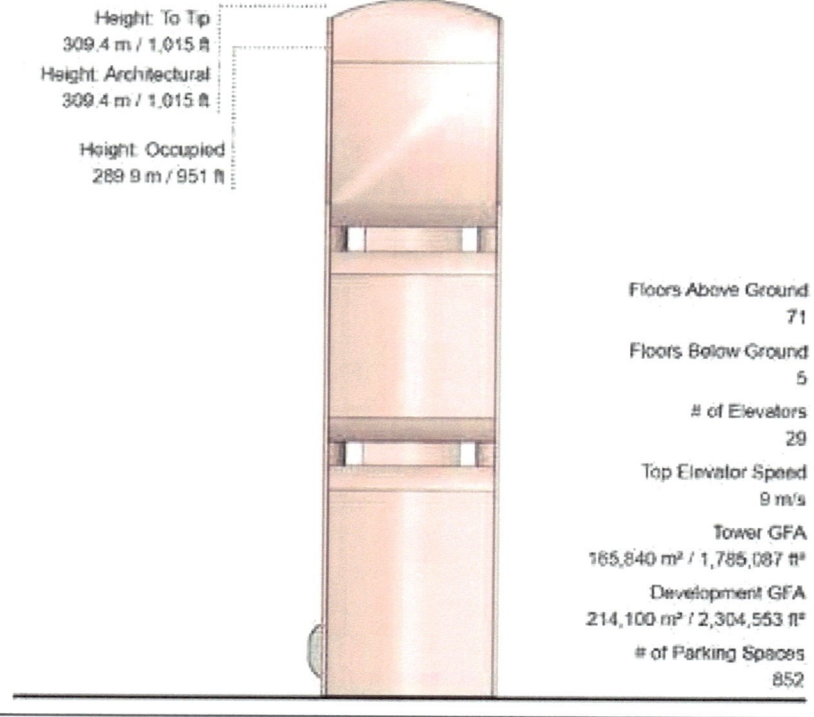

Fig. (6). Schematic of the main façade of Pearl River Tower. Courtesy of the CTBUH Skyscraper.

The original design was a rectangular building for optimal natural light utilisation. Further optimisation for wind energy harvesting was introduced by curving the vertical long sides of the rectangular building to build up more wind pressure, as shown in Fig. (**8**), which is a similar concept to that of Strata SE1. To reduce the detrimental structural loads of this added wind pressure, the building was incorporated with four openings (*i.e.* two on each mechanical floor), as shown in Figs. (**6** and **8**), passing through the building from the windward to leeward sides. Each opening measured 5 m × 4 m. Furthermore, the building façade was curved around the sides of these openings to streamline wind flow and to further reduce wind pressure on the building façade (Fig. **9**). These openings are the perfect location where the wind turbines can be integrated, considering the increased wind velocities at this location, which is the main factor of enhancement for wind energy generation using wind turbines.

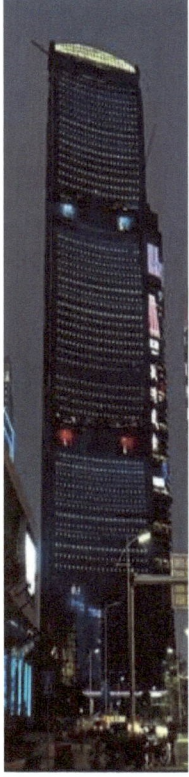

Fig. (7). Turbine's indicator lamps turning green when meeting (or exceeding) the energy demand and turning red when in deficit. Courtesy of Archello.com [14].

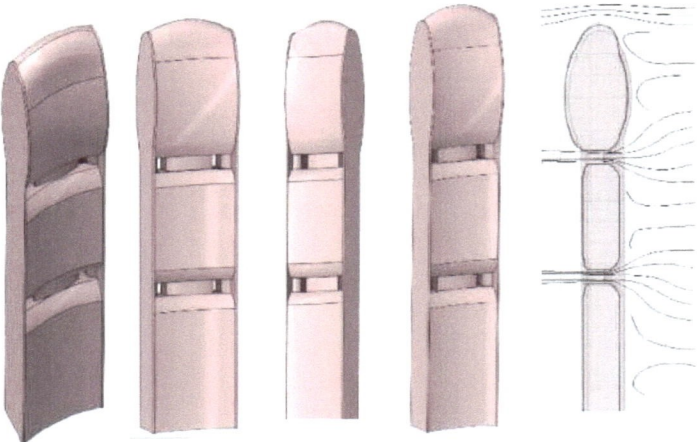

Fig. (8). Façade and plan curvature prompting wind flow through the openings. Courtesy of SOM [15].

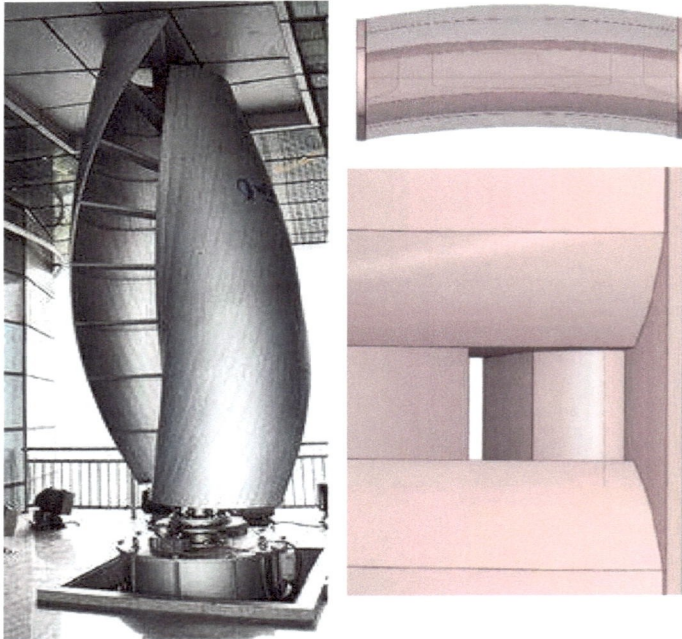

Fig. (9). The openings and turbine positions within them. Courtesy of SOM [15].

The top of the tower is also curved from above to reduce vortex shedding, which is a phenomenon that may cause destruction of tall buildings due to high wind loads (discussed in further detail in section 3.1).

The building is incorporated with four wind turbines, one for each of the four openings. Each turbine is 5-m tall and 2-m wide (Fig. **9**). The four turbines produce about 30,000 kWh of electricity each year, which is 5% of the total energy demand of the building. They are one of the most successful wind turbines integrated into tall buildings and are closely monitored. Further, they are equipped with indicator lamps on the building's façade that turn green when the generated power surpasses the demand and turn red when there is a deficit, as illustrated in Figure 7. The main takeaway is that it is inadequate both in terms of architectural soundness considering the aerodynamics of tall buildings and from the standpoint of energy production to merely incorporate wind turbines of any type into tall buildings, with the expectation of receiving the highest wind energy harvesting. Further optimisation of the architectural form is necessary in this regard.

A possible enhancement for Pearl River Tower would be the further optimisation of the wind turbine positions within the openings [13]. This is discussed further in Chapter 6.

3. WIND AND ARCHITECTURAL SAFETY

In buildings, wind is responsible for structural vibration and oscillations [16]. In particular, tall buildings are exposed to magnified and intensified wind velocities as well as flow regime. High wind velocities can exert positive pressure on the windward side of buildings and a negative pressure on the leeward side, which is referred to as the drag force. These pressures can be reduced greatly by introducing uniform dimples on the surfaces, such as those on golf balls [17]. The wind particles get 'confused' by the non-uniformity of the surface as they strike these dimples. Thus, they do not strike with the maximum force, greatly reducing the pressure on the surface. This concept allows a golf ball to travel much further. This principle could be applied to buildings' façades if the need arises.

3.1. Wind-induced Vibration in Buildings—Definition and Cause

Destructive Wind-induced vibration in tall buildings is caused by dynamic oscillations that resonate with the natural frequencies of the structures. Only very specific wind velocities can cause these oscillations for specific structures, and other architectural forms would have different wind velocities triggering such oscillations [18]. The form of a building primarily causes these dynamic oscillations and/or the symmetrical shape and dimensions of cross sections of it plans. This implies that uniform square, rectangular or cylindrical [19] forms are more prone to these oscillations, as can be seen in Figs. (**10a, 10b** and **10c**). These figures illustrate the localised wind velocities for a tall building of a square cross-section under wind-induced vibration. Fig. (**10b**) shows the separation and division of the wind flow into two coupling sections on each opposite façade. Normally, one couple has a higher velocity than the neighbouring one. With the continuous passage of wind across the building façades and at a specific wind velocity, this coupling will be strong enough to swing the building to it sides as it departs the façades of the building. When the dynamic oscillation coincides with the natural frequency of the building, the wind-induced vibrations will continue until the building collapses, *e.g.* the Tacoma Narrows Bridge collapse in 1940.

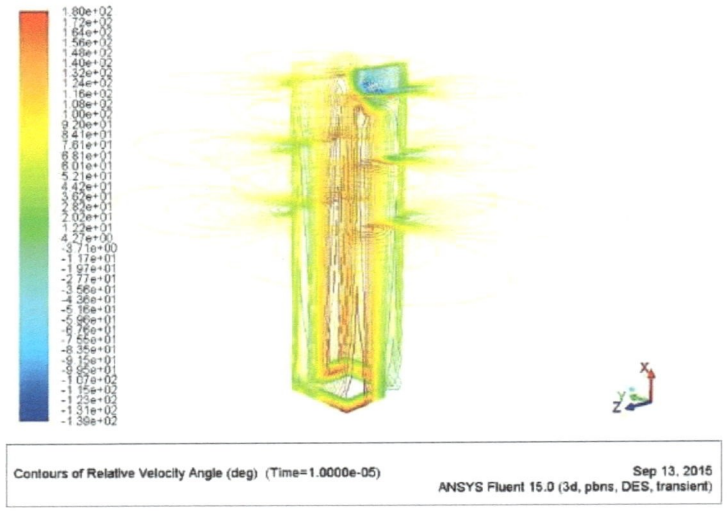

Fig. (10a). Velocity contours along and around the façades of a tall building under wind-induced vibration.

3.2. Wind-induced Vibration in Buildings—Remedies and Measures

Unlike earthquakes, wind-induced vibrations are totally triggered by the building's 3D form and/or cross-sectional uniformity. Therefore, the main strategy to mitigate wind-induced vibration in buildings is choosing the adequate form and plan configurations [20]. A good example in this regard is Burj Khalifa, a tall building in Dubai. The building tapers in the form of a Fibonacci spiral ascending plan reduced with the height of the building, thus considerably eliminating vortex shedding.

Furthermore, the impacts of wind-induced vibrations on architectural forms and their vulnerability to these vibrations have been researched by Tamura *et al* [21]. They studied a number of architectural forms that mitigate building oscillation due to wind-induced vibration based on the very strategy discussed here.

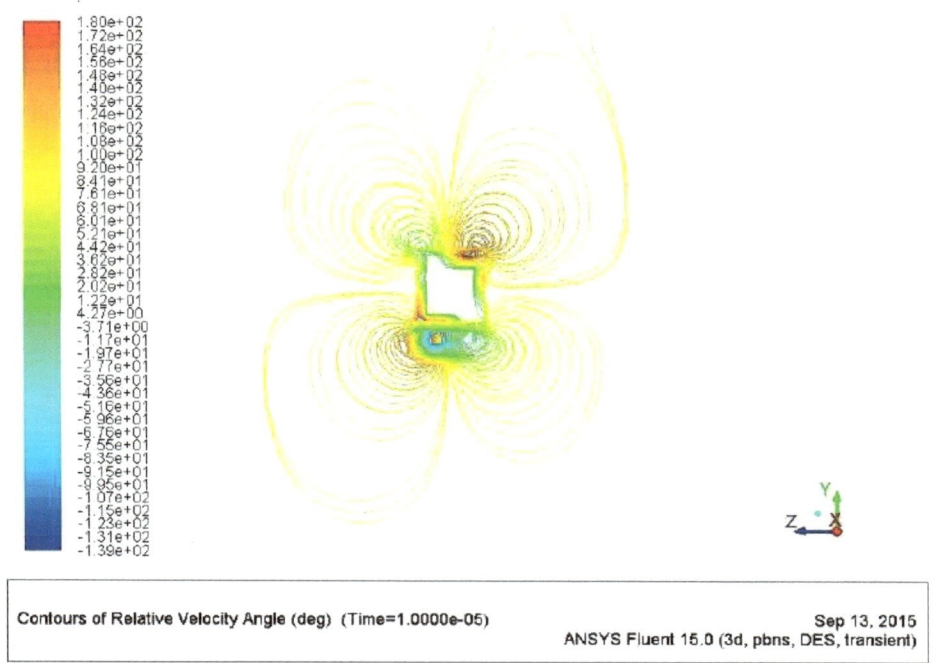

Fig. (10b). Velocity contours in the plan illustrating the coupling effect of the wind velocity just before departing the building.

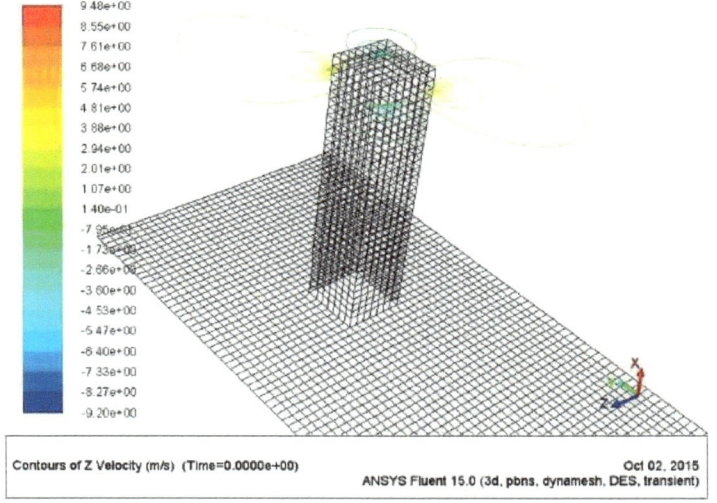

Fig. (10c). Velocity contours in 3D illustrating the coupling effect of velocity just before departing the building.

Their study comprised some alteration to the basic forms (*i.e.* square, rectangular, triangular, circular, *etc.*) of tall and super tall buildings that experienced wind-induced vibrations. Then, they introduced an element to each form to breakdown their symmetrical configuration one at a time. They introduced corner chamfer, corner cut, tri-corner cut, tilting, winding, tapered in different forms, setback, inversely tapered and bulged form. All showed plausible reductions in oscillations compared with their basic original square forms. An alternative active solution to this oscillation problem is the introduction of mechanical or structural dampers, which come in various types and forms. They are complicated systems that are difficult to design and install and are very expensive in terms of purchasing, installation and maintenance costs.

3.3. Performance Criteria for Tall Buildings under Wind Design

3.3.1. Human Comfort

The tall buildings subjected to high wind velocities can affect the human comfort in many ways. These can be due to air infiltration, heat loss due to ventilation, vibration, rain infiltration and condensation. Vibrations are the most closely related with the choice of architectural form as explained previously in sections 3.1 and 3.2. This is because people perceive the rate of movement rather than the movement itself as uncomfortable. The rate of movement is the acceleration measured in milli-g, where g is the acceleration due to gravity. This acceleration effect can be enormous for wind-induced vibrations [22].

4. BUILDING'S AERODYNAMIC PERFORMANCE

Further aerodynamic design adaptation of architectural forms based on the blending of the cross sections is discussed and the 3D comparisons of their amalgamations with the basic tall square buildings can illustrate the importance of this aspect. Tamura *et al* [21] tested some of these architectural forms under direct and cross winds using CFD as well as wind tunnel models.

The models examined are basic forms including square, rectangle, circle, ellipse, tilted, snaked and winded, along with corner modifications such as tapered, bulged and helical openings all in different modifications and finally composite forms (Table **1**). There are a total of 31 models in seven categories (additional six models by the author mentioned here). Tamura *et al* obtained the values of the local mean wind force coefficient using CFD, overturning moment coefficient, CMD, CML and fluctuating overturning moment coefficient in the cross wind, along wind and torsional directions CMT (Fig. **11**). In addition, the wind pressure coefficient, Cp, and response analysis were also assessed for these models. Eigenvalue analysis and response analysis were conducted to determine the habitability of the studied models. Helical and corner-cut models had the safest habitability, aerodynamics response and structural stability as they exhibited the lowest spectral wind velocities for one-year return period far better than those of the basic square model. A resemblance with these results is evident in models with extra helical angles even with better results. However, the setbacks experienced larger spectral wind velocities than the original basic square form, producing minimal wind pressures due to the reduced surface area, thus jeopardising their expected safe habitability. This proves that aerodynamic modifications can lead to the improvement of stability of structures and elimination of vortex shedding when carefully devised to do so.

Table 1. Tested and proposed building forms for combating wind-induced vibrations.

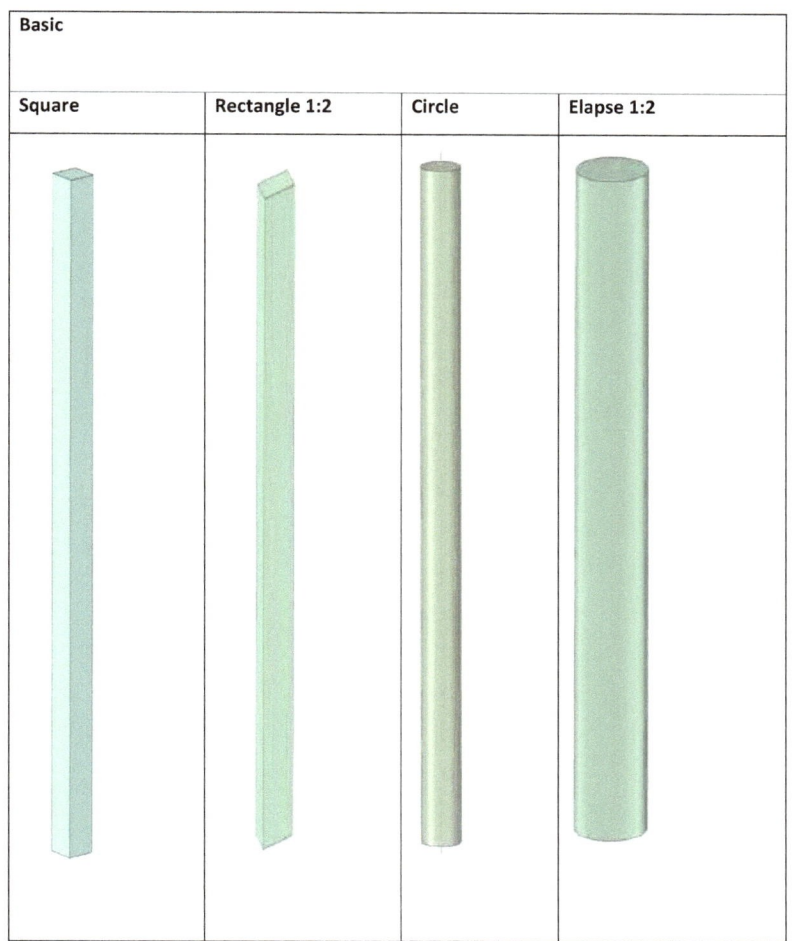

(Table 1) cont.....

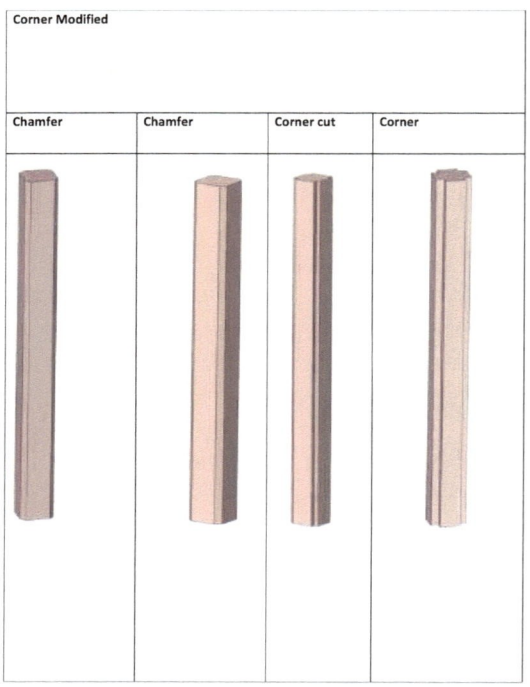

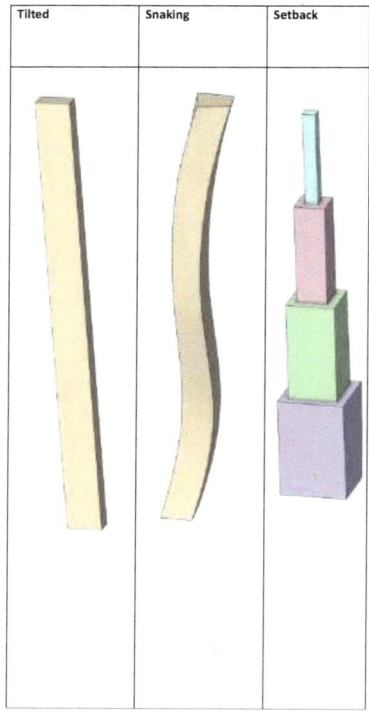

Tapered			
Tapered -1	Tapered -2	Tapered-3	Bulged

(Table 1) cont.....

Helical			
Helical Square 90°	Helical Square 180°	Helical Square 270°	Helical Square 360°
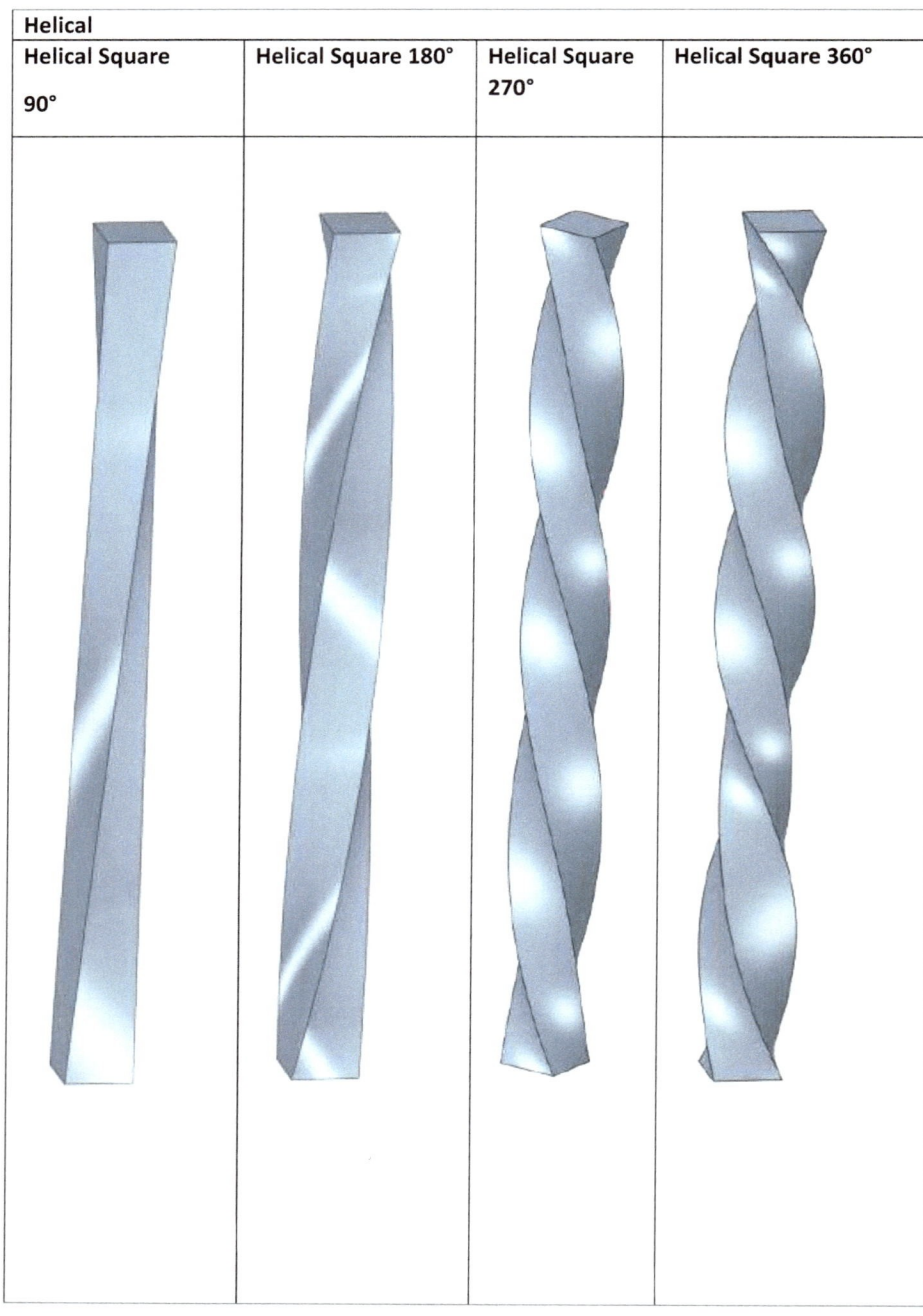			

(Table 1) cont.....

Helical Composite				
Circular Helical 90°	Circular+ Rectanglar+ Helical 90°	Rectangular + Helical 90°	Eleptical+ Helical 180°	Rectangular + Helical 180°

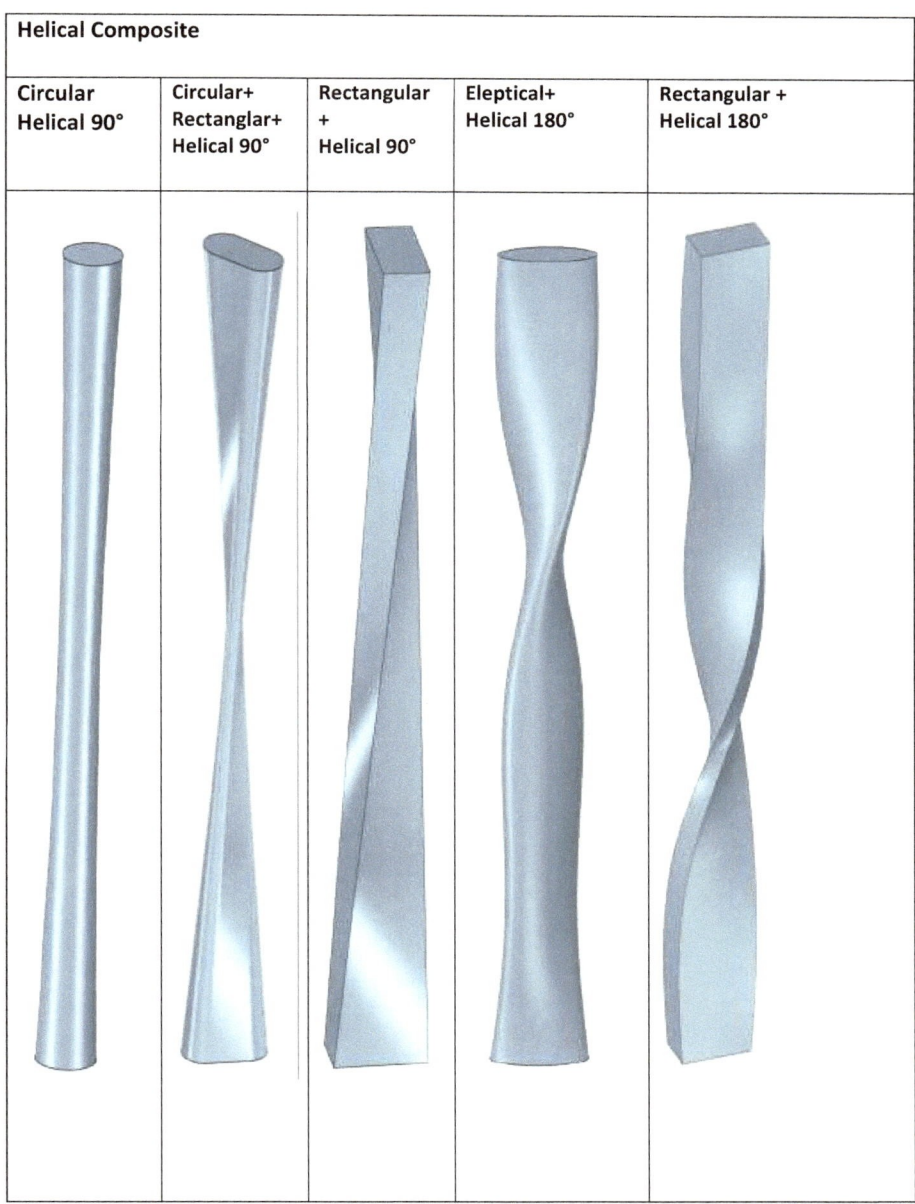

(Table 1) cont.....

Opening			
Cross Void	Cross Void	Cross Void	3-Circles

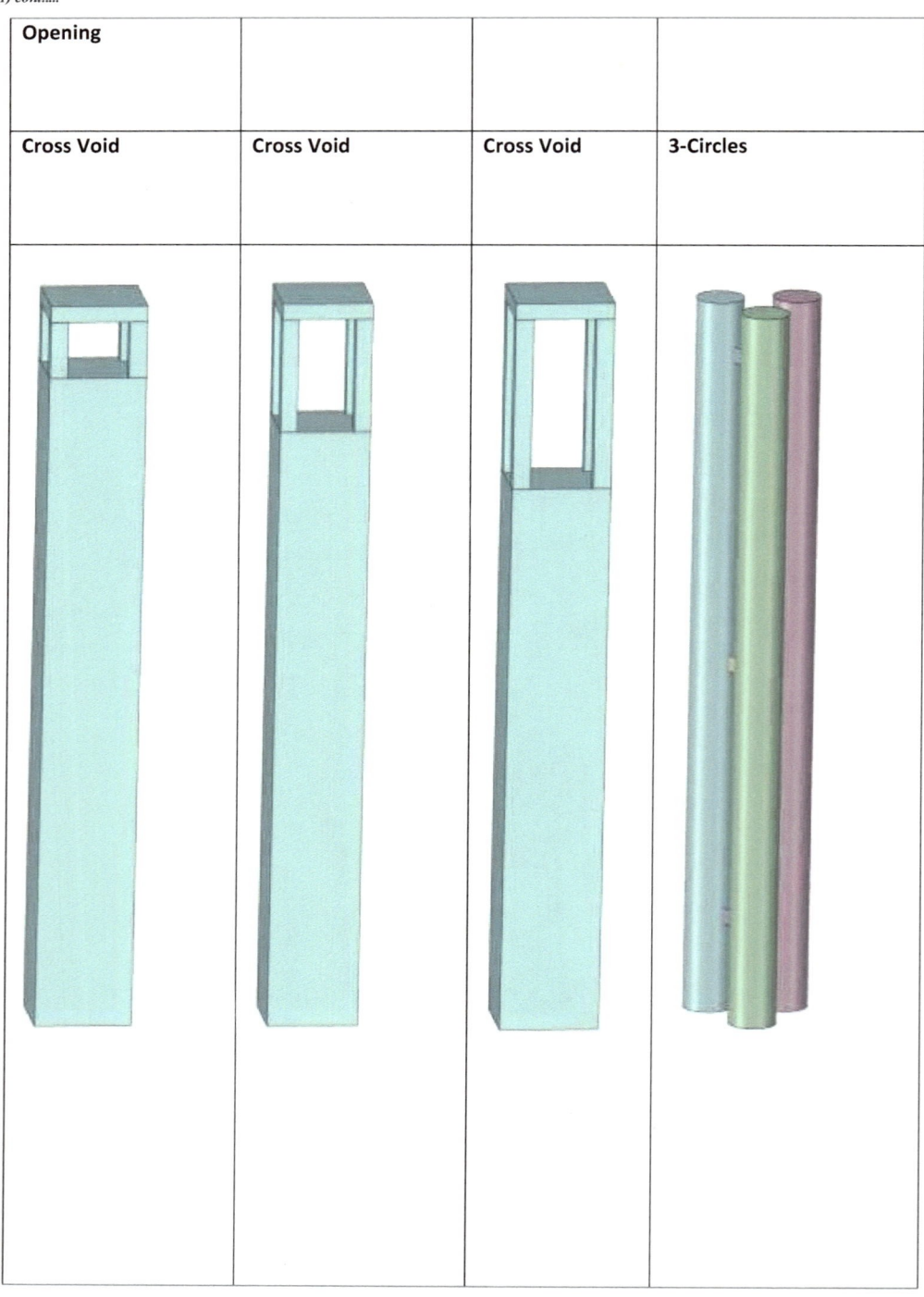

(Table 1) cont.....

Corner Cut Oblique Void	Oblique Void	Oblique Void
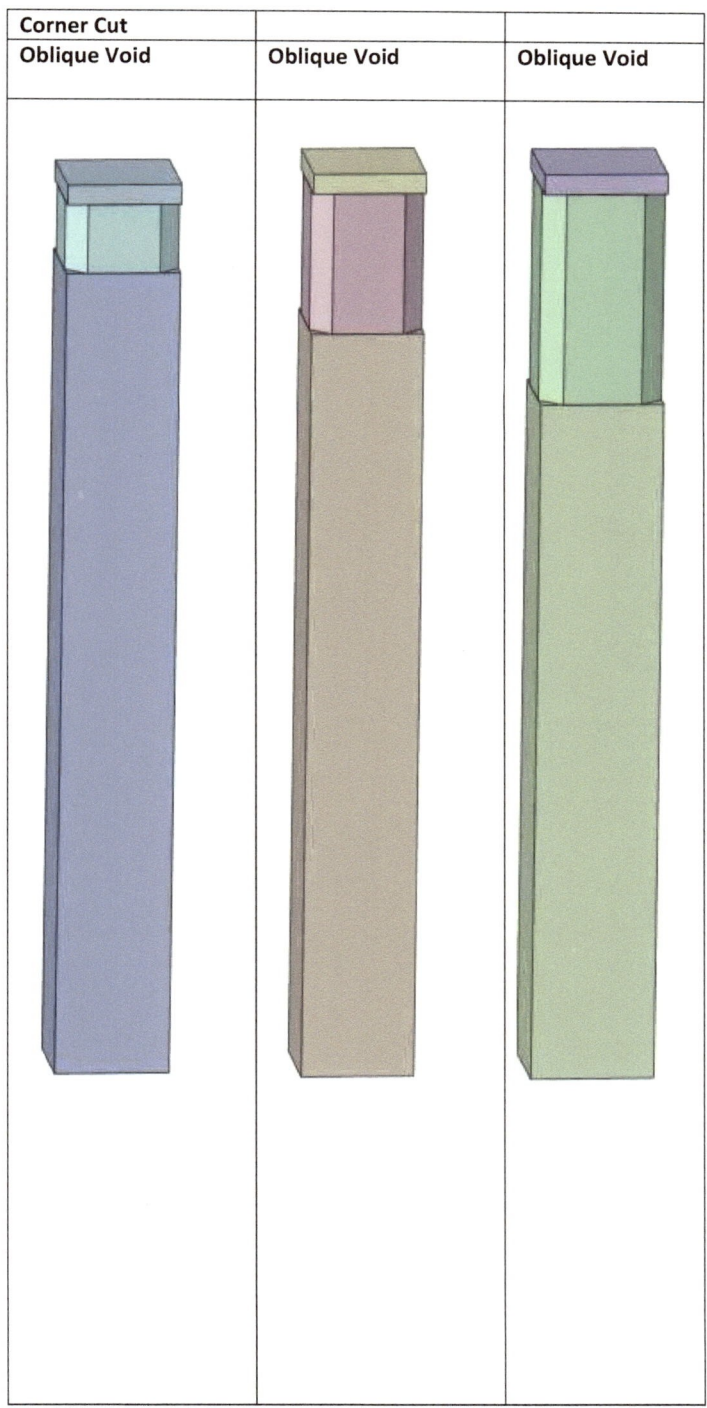		

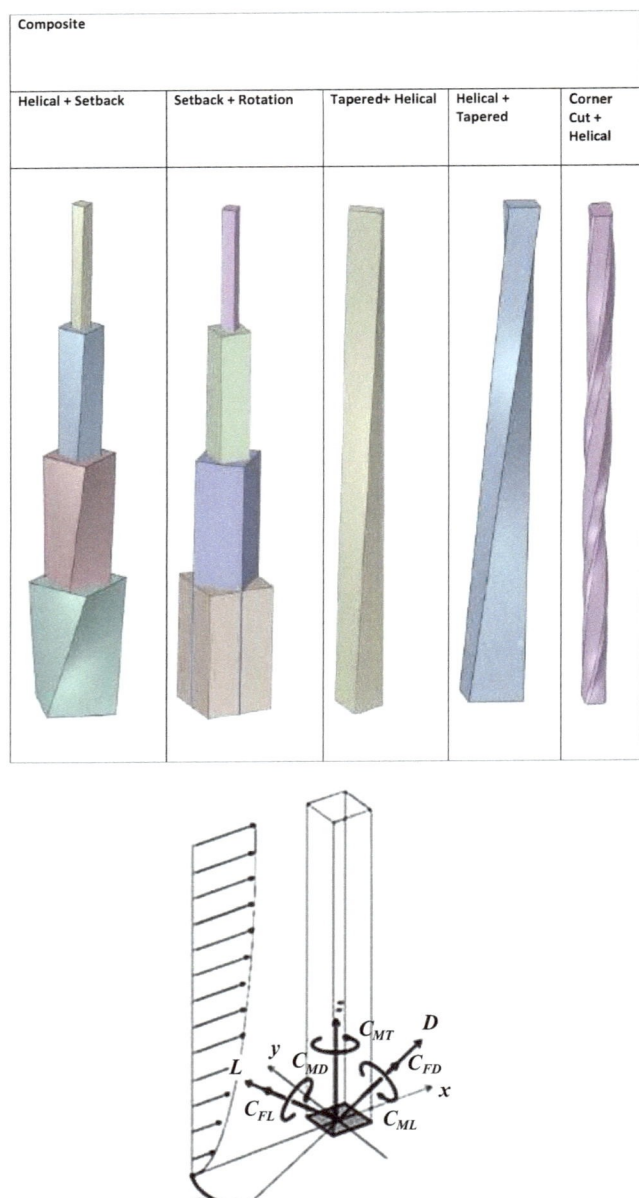

Fig. (11). Aerodynamic forces acting on a basic tall square building. Courtesy of Tamura *et al* [21].

CONCLUSION

- Architectural forms can fully control a building's structural stability through the choice and optimisation of the aerodynamic performance.

- Not optimising architectural forms aerodynamically may render the buildings susceptible to huge costs needed for employing active structural or mechanical damping measures and solutions.

- Architectural forms for incorporating wind energy generation can be gauged, optimised and compared by determining the capacity factors.

- Causes of vortex shedding in tall buildings are determined and measures for their resolution are divulged. Namely, the uniformity of the vertical and horizontal cross sections of buildings should be treated with a variety of architectural forms of unsymmetrical configurations.

- Some notably aerodynamically stable forms of tall buildings are proposed with qualities that distinguish them based on their pronounced vortex shedding combating measures. Rotational building shapes exhibited the safest aerodynamic behaviour under wind tunnel and CFD simulations.

REFERENCES

[1] J. Rao, *Wind Mills.*, 2011, pp. 13-14.

[2] M. Kazemi Esfeh, A. A. Dehghan, and M. Dehghan Manshadi, "Wind-catchers, creative buildings' elements for passive ventilation", *Advances in Energy Research and Development,* vol. 6, pp. 189-222, 2021.

[3] T. Stathopoulos, and C. Baniotopoulos, *Wind Effects on Buildings and Design of Wind-Sensitive Structures.* Springer-Verlag Wien, 2007.
[http://dx.doi.org/10.1007/978-3-211-73076-8]

[4] N. Sakhri, Y. Menni, H. Ameur, A. Chamkha, K. Noureddine, M. Bensafi, G. Lorenzini, and O. Makinde, "Investigation of the natural ventilation of wind catchers with different geometries in arid region houses", *Journal of Mechanical Engineering and Sciences,* vol. 14, pp. 7109-7124, 2020.
[http://dx.doi.org/10.15282/jmes.14.3.2020.12.0557]

[5] B.D, "Architect of the Z-factory sustainable project", *His practise BedZEd,* 2020. http://www.soetownsville.org/external_pages/SkyZED_The_Flower_Tower.html

[6] N. Campbell, S. Stankovic, J.M.R. Graham, P. Parkin, M. Duijvendijk, T. Gruiter, S. Behling, J. Hieber, and M.J. Blanch, "Wind Energy For The Built Environment", In: *Proceedings of the 2001 European wind energy conference, Copenhagen, Denmark* Project Web, 2020, pp. 112-115.

[7] D. Taylor, "Using buildings to harvest wind energy", *Build. Res. Inform.,* vol. 26, no. 3, pp. 199-202, 1998.
[http://dx.doi.org/10.1080/096132198369977]

[8] R. Smith, and S. Killa, "Bahrain world trade center(BWTC): The first large-scale integration of wind turbines in a building", *The structural design of tall and special buildings,* vol. 16, no. 4, pp. 429-439, 2007.
[http://dx.doi.org/410.1002/tal.1416]

[9] A.A. Elmokadem, N.A. Megahed, and D.S. Noaman, "Systematic framework for the efficient integration of wind technologies into buildings", *Frontiers of Architectural Research,* vol. 5, no. 1, pp. 1-14, 2016.

[10] I. Angulo, D. De La Vega, and Ã. Casc, "Impact analysis of wind farms on telecommunication services", In: *Renewable and Sustainable Energy Reviews* vol. 32. , 2014, pp. 84-99.

[11] W. Baker, C. Besjak, B. McElhatten, and X. Li, "Pearl River Tower: Design Integration towards", *Sustainability,* 2014.

[12] A.R. Elbakheit, "Effect of turbine resistance and positioning on performance of Aerofoil wing building augmented wind energy generation", *Energy Build.,* vol. 174, pp. 365-371, 2018.
[http://dx.doi.org/10.1016/j.enbuild.2018.06.025]

[13] Archello.com, Accedded October 2020, *Pearl's river tower wind turbines energy generation indicator.*

[14] SOM website, Accessed, *Pearl river tower,* 2020.

[15] A. Lago, D. Trabucco, and A. Wood, *Damping considerations in tall buildings," Damping Technologies for Tall Buildings.,* A. Lago, D. Trabucco, A. Wood, Eds., Butterworth-Heinemann, 2019, pp. 39-106.
[http://dx.doi.org/10.1016/B978-0-12-815963-7.00003-8]

[16] C.H. Tai, C.Y. Chao, and J. Leong, "Effects of golf ball dimple configuration on aerodynamics, trajectory, and acoustics", *Journal of Flow Visualization and Image Processing,* vol. 14, pp. 183-200, 2007.
[http://dx.doi.org/10.1615/JFlowVisImageProc.v14.i2.40]

[17] A. R. Elbakheit, *Wind-Induced Vibrations to Tall Buildings and Wind Turbines.,* 2018.
[http://dx.doi.org/10.5772/intechopen.72094]

[18] T. Li, and J.Y.Z. Zhang, "Vortex-Induced Vibration Characteristics of an Elastic Circular Cylinder", *World Academy of Science, Engineering and Technology,* 2009.

[19] Y.C. Kim, J. Kanda, and Y. Tamura, "Wind-induced coupled motion of tall buildings with varying square plan with height", *J. Wind Eng. Ind. Aerodyn.,* vol. 99, no. 5, pp. 638-650, 2011.
[http://dx.doi.org/10.1016/j.jweia.2011.03.004]

[20] T.e.a., "Aerodynamic and flow characteristics of tall buildings with various unconventional configurations", *International High-rise Building Journal,* vol. 2, no. 3, 2013.

[21] T. Balendra, "Aerodynamic and flow characteristics of tall buildings with various unconventional configurations", *Vibration of Buildings to Wind and Earthquake Loads.,* 1993.
[http://dx.doi.org/10.1007/978-1-4471-2055-1]

CHAPTER 2

Aerodynamic Architectural Design

Abstract: This chapter attempts to scan various wind aerodynamic responses relevant to buildings that could be utilised for wind energy generation. It highlights some natural ventilation mechanisms and processes that allow continuous air streams amenable to further streamlining for wind energy generation. This study analyses various types of flows and their characteristics. Further streamlining of architectural forms to generate optimal wind flows prior to energy harvesting is discussed.

Keywords: Aerodynamic architectural design, Aerofoils, Aerofoil optimisation, Bernoulli effect, Venturi effect, Wind flow types.

1. INTRODUCTION

Aerodynamic design is a well-established term when it comes to the designs of most transportation means such as cars, trains, ships, and planes. However, apart from planes, only the very high-end products of the other means of transportation are actually designed considering the aerodynamics. This is basically due to the high influence of aerodynamic design on the performance required from racing cars, for instance, wherein air drag and resistance must be exceptionally low, and stability and safety are paramount.

In contrast, for buildings, wind interaction, especially in terms of the design of the building, is normally kept to a minimum either because of the requirement for natural ventilation or because it is stipulated by codes for structural safety and quality of life or comfort. However, for harvesting wind energy as a sustainable energy source at the point where it is made, building design needs to adapt, and therefore, an aerodynamic version of the architectural design must follow suit with high-end transportation means.

The terms aerodynamic architectural design and dynamic design are used in architectural designs to justify ideas that are normally outside the box or more curvilinear and organic in shape. In wind physics, this is not far from the truth;

however, the air movement mechanisms around buildings are the same regardless of whether the architectural form is curvilinear, organic, or square. However, organic forms may pose less resistance to wind flow.

In nature, wind is produced by various means, such as the Earth's rotation around its axis and temperature differences, which subsequently lead to pressure differences, giving birth to natural convection currents. Air moves from high-pressure to low-pressure regions [1]. These pressure differences are caused by temperature changes in the air due to solar radiation heating of large amounts of land, which, in turn, heats the adjoining air just above the surface. Hot air is less dense and rises, and cooler, denser air descends to take its place. This principle applies to air at all levels in the entire atmosphere, which is hundreds of thousands of kilometres to small rooms, which are several metres in length.

When wind strikes a building's external surfaces, it either separates, accelerates or recirculates, with all three happening simultaneously on the same building, but at different surfaces depending on which surface is facing the wind in which direction. Naturally, only acceleration of wind is favourable for wind energy generation, while recirculation is detrimental. We try to explain some mechanisms that can foster good quality wind for energy generation in the following sections.

2. REASONS FOR AERODYNAMIC ARCHITECTURAL DESIGN

2.1. Ventilation

Ventilation is vital for maintaining freshness, health, and well-being in addition to cooling. Ventilation is needed inside buildings both in summer and winter. In summer, it can further improve passive cooling mechanisms. However, natural ventilation has some limits when it comes to satisfying human comfort to the fullest level. In contrast, unwanted ventilation in winter, where external cold wind infiltrates into the building and is called infiltration, negatively impacts the efficiency of heating systems. A simple solution to this is improving airtightness and seals of windows, fenestrations and other openings. Generally, in buildings, ventilation depends on a number of different factors highlighted in the following sections.

2.1.1. Natural Wind Pressure

Natural wind pressure provides the main general pattern of wind flow at a location. The cityscape generally comes within the natural atmospheric boundary layer, as shown in Fig. (**1**), which contains high wind velocities in the upper levels of the boundary layer and low wind velocities in the lower level, *i.e.* near the ground and around the buildings [2]. However, each building would be more influenced by the structures in its immediate vicinity, such as adjoining buildings and vegetation. Sections 3.4–3.6 highlight simulation studies on the boundary layer around buildings in more detail.

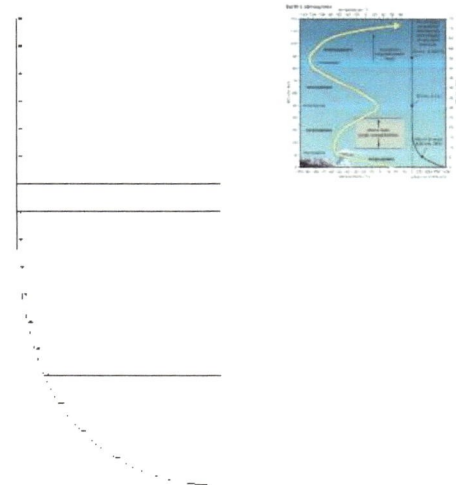

Fig. (1). Natural boundary layer of the atmosphere [3].

2.1.2. Displacement or Stack Ventilation

Displacement ventilation inside buildings occurs due to temperature difference between the lower and higher levels. Therefore, in tall buildings or atriums the stack effect is much more pronounced compared to that in low-rise or short buildings, wherein air stratification in layers of different temperatures become more pronounced. This is an area where many utilisations of this phenomenon exists. This is valid for chimney stacks, exhaust flues to solar collectors and chimneys. The main concern for this is not to mix stack ventilation with fire exits and routes because this would bring fire and flammable gases into what is presumably designed to be a safe exit from fire.

Similarly, for wind energy generation, a vertical stack has to be devoted to this purpose only, where we can generate appreciable wind velocity from vertical shafts that accelerate wind velocity with virtue of its height, obviously to levels beyond the comfort level of the occupants. The taller the building, the higher the resulting wind velocities will be [4]. Such vertical air movement can be even more enhanced with the introduction of more buoyancy of the air by heating it *via* solar radiation as in solar chimneys or heated vertical ducts [5, 6]. This accelerated wind can be harvested as a renewable energy source using wind turbines.

The airflow induced by the stack effect can be expressed as follows [7]:

$$Q\text{ stack} = cdA\sqrt{\frac{2gh\,(Ti-To)}{Ti}}, \qquad (1)$$

where Ti is the average temperature of indoor air (K), T_o is the average temperature of outdoor air (K), Q stack is the volume of ventilation rate (m³/s), Cd is the discharge coefficient, 0.65, A is the free area of the inlet opening (m²), which equals area of the outlet opening, g is the acceleration due to gravity, 9.8 m/s², h is the vertical distance between the inlet and outlet midpoints (m).

2.1.3. Bernoulli Effect

Bernoulli effect [8] states that when air velocity increases, the static pressure decreases.

2.1.4. Venturi Tube

Venturi effect [9] states that when air passes through a restriction, its velocity increases. This is clear from the Venturi tube shown in Fig. (2), wherein the tube contains a wide entrance and exit, but a restriction in the middle.

Considering the building's applications, when applying the Bernoulli effect to the Venturi tube (Fig. 3), we can see that a negative pressure would result from this increase in velocity, and therefore, air would be drawn in from inside the tower and rooms at lower levels towards the negative pressure at the top of tower, as shown in Fig. (4).

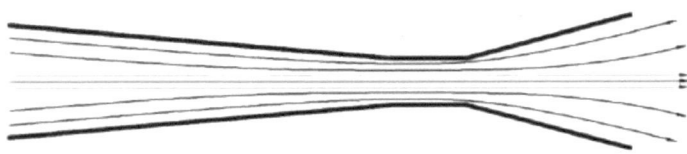

Fig. (2). Venturi tube with a restriction in the middle, which accelerates the air.

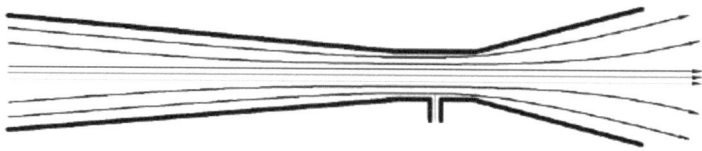

Fig. (3). Venturi tube with an opening in the middle of the restriction to draw in more air from below.

Fig. (4). A ventilation tower drawing air from lower-level rooms using Venturi and Bernoulli effects to enhance the stack effect.

2.1.5. Types of Wind Flows: Laminar, Separated, Turbulent or Eddy Flows

Laminar flow (Fig. **5**) refers to a homogeneous and streamlined flow, lacking any swirls, turns or eddies. Separated flow (Fig. **6**) is flow that is divided into two or more streams.

Fig. (5). Laminar flow.

Fig. (6). Separated flow.

Turbulent flow (Fig. **7**) is flow that turns into chaotic and disturbed movement of particles in a certain region. Reynold's number (Re), which is a dimensionless number, is often employed to verify whether a flow is laminar, turbulent or transitional (*i.e.* in between laminar and turbulent).

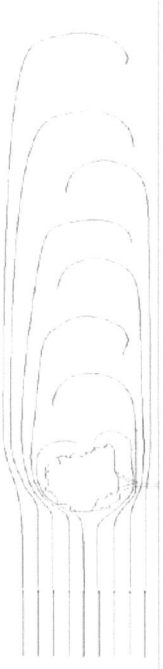

Fig. (7). Turbulent flow.

Re [10] can be calculated using the following equation:

$$Re = \frac{\rho v L}{\mu} \qquad (2)$$

where

ρ is the density of the fluid (kg/m³), v is a characteristic velocity of the fluid with respect to the object (m/s), L is a characteristic linear dimension (m), and μ is the dynamic viscosity of the fluid (Pa·s or N·s/m² or kg/(m·s)).

Generally speaking, when the Re is less than 2300, the flow is laminar, between 2300 and 4000, the flow is transient, greater than 4000, the flow is turbulent.

2.1.6. Air Inertia

Air has weight and therefore behaves accordingly.

2.1.7. No Vacuum in the Atmosphere

Air can neither be created nor destroyed.

3. WIND ENERGY HARVESTING

3.1. Building Design Optimisation for Potential Wind Energy Collection

3.1.1. Overview

Numerous research studies on wind flows around buildings have been conducted *via* testing and simulations. As a result of these studies, for a rectangular [11] building facing direct wind flow or sloped [12] roof sides facing direct wind, the wind velocities just above the architectural form speed up. Flow separation across a section of the building occurs under the effect of the wind being divulged (Fig. **8**). It is clear that wind separates at the top of the building with areas of turbulence at the back of the building and positive pressure in front of the building.

The total picture of the wind flow around a building (Fig. **8**) reveals that the flow would be separated at the top of the building with areas of positive pressure in front of the building.

Regions of swirls present at the top and back of the building as well as at the foot of the building from the front or windward sides. The flow separates around the building at each sharp edge and produces swirls and eddies.

This separation owing to the building obstructing the flow also accelerates the wind flow at the top of the building.

Many researchers have studied this separation phenomenon in an attempt to pinpoint the precise locations and limits of the swirls and eddies around the obstructing bodies in relation to their geometrical dimensions and Reynolds stresses [13, 14].

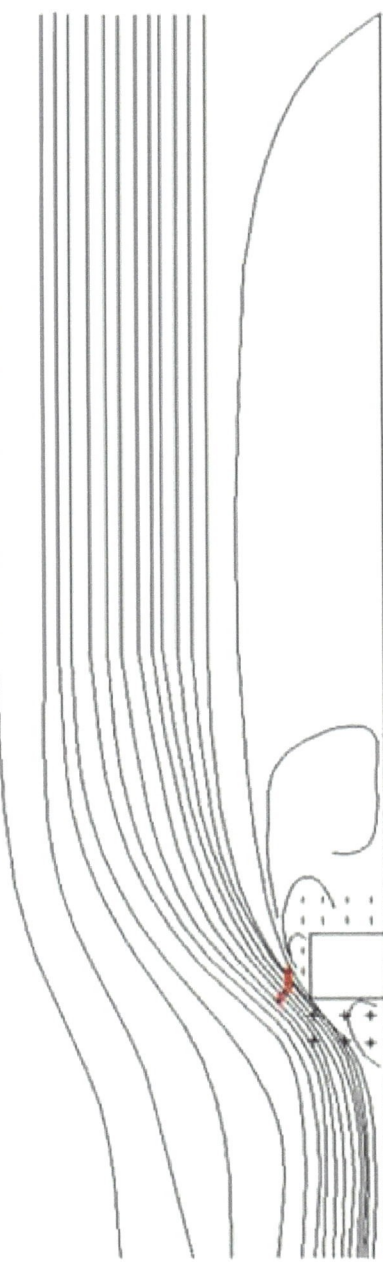

Fig. (8). Schematic sketch of the flow, with areas of recirculation in front and at the top and back of the building (left to right). + Positive Pressure − Negative pressure.

For the study on aerodynamic design for wind energy generation, only the acceleration part of wind separation along the edges of buildings is important. This is because buildings that are positioned in the wake of other taller buildings would be deprived of the acceleration effect because they would be subjected to swirls (*i.e.* turbulence) caused by buildings in prior contact with the wind as illustrated in Fig. (**9**). Only if the buildings possess sufficient height to elevate them outside the boundaries of the recirculations or swirls, they would benefit from this phenomenon.

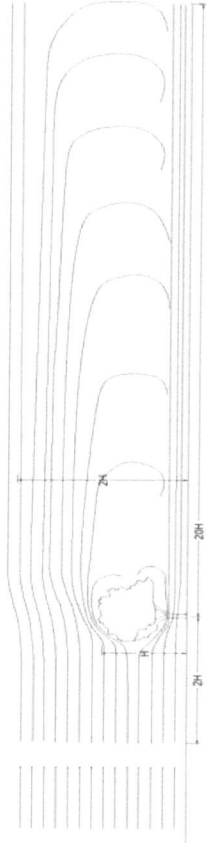

Fig. (9). Projected areas where recirculation takes place.

As depicted in Fig. (**9**), when a laminar flow of air is obstructed by a building of height H, at the leeward side, the flow would develop into turbulence and recirculation flows to a height equalling twice the height of the obstacle and to a distance equalling 20-times the height of the obstacle on the leeward side.

3.2. Aerodynamic Aerofoils for Wind Energy Generation

Wind separation owing to buildings and other obstacles provide one of the most promising opportunities to harvest wind energy into valuable electricity in the built environment. However, how to benefit from aerodynamic aerofoils for wind energy generation and what qualities of the aerofoils could be optimised to achieve better energy generation are questions that must be answered.

An attempt is to use this separation/acceleration by using building-integrated wind turbines. This accelerated flow can be further enhanced by the incorporation of aerofoils at specific locations around the building.

Factors affecting the performance of aerofoils are as follows [15]:

1. The distance of the aerofoil from the roof; D in Fig. (**10**).
2. The opening angle of the aerofoil (angle of attack); angle A in Fig. (**10**).

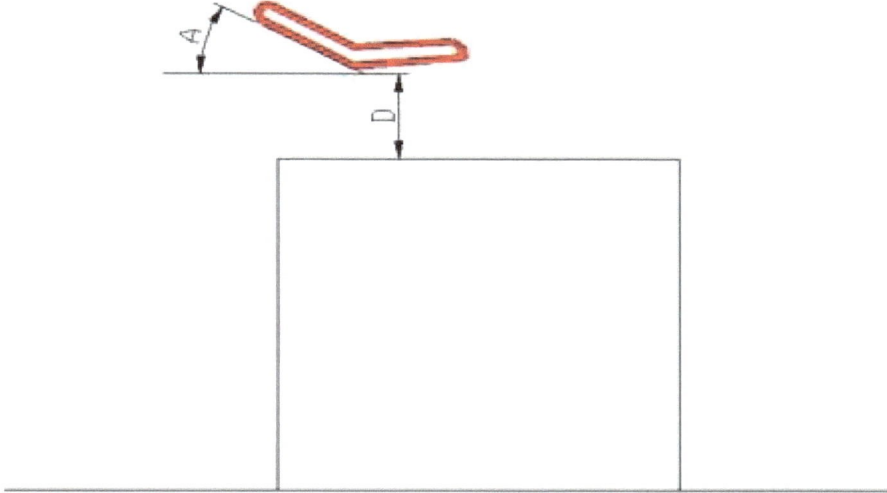

Fig. (10). Two-dimensional schematic of the main parameters affecting the performance of an aerofoil on top of a building.

Positioning the aerofoil on top of buildings further enhanced resulting wind velocities particularly in the region below the aerofoil with added streamlining of the flow. The aerofoil by virtue of aforementioned factors of proximity to roof and angle of attack would accelerate the air flow rate by concentrating large amounts of air through a restriction, thus reducing swirls and turbulence in this region. Therefore, aerofoils can increase the potential of successful wind energy harvesting. However, the aerofoils must be properly anchored as they would be subjected to large drag forces and uplifting. Fig. (**11**) reveals the predicted flow distribution after installation of the aerofoil on top of the building.

Fig. (11). Two-dimensional schematic of the flow separation after installing a an aerofoil on top of a building.

The acceleration effect is shown in Fig. (**11**) by the virtue of the flow lines accumulating, congesting and streamlining in their course across and over the building. This is due to the fact that for an incompressible fluid flow, the product of the cross-sectional area and velocity at any position in the passing fluid remains constant.

$$V_1 A_1 = V_2 A_2 = V_n A_n \quad (3)$$

where V is the flow velocity and A is the cross-sectional area. From equation 3, the velocity V can be increased to as high a value as required by reducing the area A accordingly.

A hose of running water subjected to slight pressure or a restriction at its outlet follows the same principle, *i.e.* a reciprocating increase in flow velocity will result to compensate for the reduction in cross-sectional area.

An additional possibility to maximise the yield of acceleration is by reducing the resistance to the flow by providing a curved façade to the architectural form on the windward side Fig. (**12**). This would streamline the flow and reduce or eliminate turbulence on the windward side, thus rendering the flow more laminar, which has the highest yield in wind energy generation.

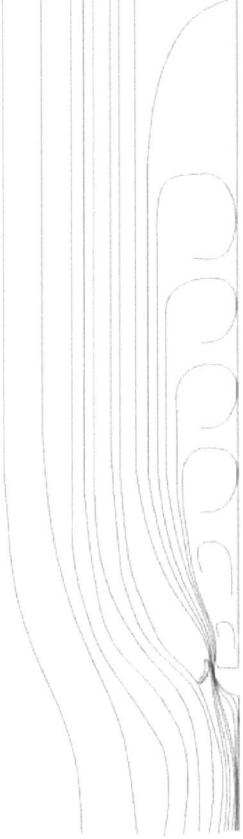

Fig. (12). Curved façade on the windward side, streamlining the flow and reducing the turbulence.

CONCLUSION

- Buildings could benefit from several wind physical phenomena for both natural ventilation and wind energy generation.

- Wind separation around corners in the built-up areas provides opportunities for accelerated wind flows that could be harvested using suitable technology.

- However, wind separation also would create areas of varying pressure distributions and other unfavourable conditions such as uplifting, turbulence, suctions or different pressures on the building's external surfaces that could hinder wind energy generation. Therefore, careful choices of shapes and profile that reduce wind loss, friction and drag are necessary for controlled separation.

- Venturi effect, Bernoulli effect and stack effect are possible mechanisms that after careful consideration can be employed to produce continuous streams of air optimised for wind energy generation in buildings.

- Aerofoils could be a valuable asset in streamlining wind separation around buildings and therefore could assist wind turbines in receiving the laminar flow of wind, which is needed for successful operation.

- Wind gets accelerated between aerofoils and buildings owing to the reduction in cross-sectional area as supported by the following product remaining constant of incompressible fluids:

$$V_1 A_1 = V_2 A_2 = V_n A_n \qquad (3)$$

Therefore, the velocity V can be increased to the maximum required extent by reducing the area A accordingly.

REFERENCES

[1] J.A. Mason, and H. de Blij, *Physical Geography: The Global Environment.* Oxford University Press, 2016.

[2] V. Spiridonov, and M. Ćurić, "Atmospheric Pressure and Wind", In: *Fundamentals of Meteorology* Springer, Cham, 2021, pp. 87-114.

[3] E. Britannica, *Layers of Earth's atmosphere,* 2020. https://www.britannica.com/science/atmosphere/Troposphere#/media/1/41364/99826

[4] A.R. Elbakheit, "Effect of duct width in ducted photovoltaic façades", *Proc. CTBUH,* 2008 pp. 795-801

[5] A. R. Elbakheit, "A Ducted Photovoltaic Facade Unit with Buoyancy Cooling: Part I Experiment", *Buildings,* vol. 9, p. 4., 2019.
[http://dx.doi.org/10.3390/buildings9040088]

[6] A.R. Elbakheit, "A Ducted Photovoltaic Façade Unit with Buoyancy Cooling: Part II CFD Simulation", *Buildings,* vol. 9, no. 5, p. 133, 2019.
[http://dx.doi.org/10.3390/buildings9050133]

[7] CIBSE, AM10: Natural ventilation in non-domestic buildings (2005).

[8] B. Daniel, "Hydrodynamica, Britannica Online Encyclopedia", *Accessed,* vol. 2, p. 7, 2020.

[9] J. Anderson, *Fundamentals of Aerodynamics.* 6th ed. McGraw-Hill Education: New York, NY, 2017.

[10] A. Sommerfeld, A Contribution to Hydrodynamic Explanation of Turbulent Fluid Motions, 1908, P. 116–124. White, Frank. *Fluid Mechanics*. 4th edition. McGraw-Hill Higher Education, 2002, ISBN: 0-07-228192-8.

[11] S. Mertens, *Wind Description for Roof Location of Wind Turbines, A design guideline or the required height of a wind turbine on a horizontal roof of a mid- to high-rise building.* Proc Global Windpower, Paris: France, 2002.

[12] P.J. Oliveira, and B.A. Younis, "On the prediction of turbulent flows around full-scale buildings", *J. Wind Eng. Ind. Aerodyn.,* vol. 86, no. 2, pp. 203-220, 2000.
[http://dx.doi.org/10.1016/S0167-6105(00)00011-8]

[13] H. Schlichting, *Boundary-Layer Theory.* McGraw Hill: New York, 1979.

[14] J.A. Peterka, R.N. Meroney, and K.M. Kothari, "Wind flow patterns about buildings", *J. Wind Eng. Ind. Aerodyn.,* vol. 21, no. 1, pp. 21-38, 1985.
[http://dx.doi.org/10.1016/0167-6105(85)90031-5]

[15] A.R. Elbakheit, "Factors enhancing aerofoil wings for wind energy harnessing in buildings", *Build. Serv. Eng. Res. Tech.,* vol. 35, no. 4, pp. 417-437, 2014.
[http://dx.doi.org/10.1177/0143624413509097]

CHAPTER 3

Wind as an On-site Energy Source

Abstract: This chapter presents tools and indicators that quantify available wind energy resources on site at global, regional, and territorial levels with passable accuracy. It gives some hints of wind availability locally for areas up to 10×10 km^2. Areas with promising energy potential are depicted clearly together with other factors contributing to the further enhancement of wind resources such as height above ground level, terrains, and off-shore areas. Moreover, this chapter sheds some light on the capacity factor and provides the means for its estimation as an indicator for the level of achievable wind energy generation enhancement at a location, rendering the value of the structures erected to harvest wind energy as a step forward towards sustainability.

Keywords: Capacity factor, Global wind atlas, High wind velocities, On-site wind quantification, Wind energy availability, Wind velocities.

1. INTRODUCTION

The quantification of wind energy resource has long been relying on metrological data gathered from stations all over the world, normally from airport weather stations, which are the most reliable sources of data for wind energy generation. These data are not always available at the point of individual sites, where they are most needed. However, wind patterns at individual sites can often be highly uncertain and intermittent. The built-up form of the urban environment is the main determinant of wind flows. Therefore, having an overview of wind profiles and patterns would be the ideal starting point. In this regard, the Global Wind Atlas [1] is highly beneficial.

For harvesting wind energy at individual sites, creating favourable opportunities based on the available conditions along with the right choices and further optimisation of architectural forms are essential. It is vital to yearn for realising continuous laminar flows as divulged in Chapters 2 and 4.

Wind energy [2] is generated using mechanical turbines that drive electric generators to produce electricity. Moreover, wind energy is an inconsistent source of power [3]. Therefore, wind energy needs to be supplemented with other sources of power generation, such as batteries, solar energy, hydropower, thermal power or even fossil fuels. Regardless, wind energy is one of the cleanest sources of energy production with little negative impact on the environment.

2. WIND ENERGY AVAILABILITY

Globally, wind energy has well-established flow patterns [4] considering the geographical locations and timing of the year. Although this (*i.e.*, flow pattern) would be a major stimulant for any particular location, any site can be considered unique in terms of its potential to harvest wind energy [5]. This is particularly evident in urban terrains compared to rural areas because the presence of building clusters, tall or short, trees and other obstructions are detrimental for wind directions, flows and velocities. However, unlike solar energy, wind energy can be available all times of the day, if the relevant measures are taken to reduce the effect of obstructions and to carefully design the required architectural forms.

The World Bank has funded an international database for wind energy potential for every region on Earth called the Global Wind Atlas (Fig. **1**). This database is an online platform available to the general public to download the prevailing statistical data on the wind velocities, wind direction, energy density, mean power density and capacity factor at a range of heights from the ground. The data are quite accurate obtained using a simulation software that has been verified and tested. However, it is not suitable for accurate simulations in areas less than 10×10 km^2 plots, where on-site measurements are preferable.

Fig. (**2**) represents the mean power density per square metre globally at a height of 100 m above ground level, where 10% of the windiest areas have a potential of wind energy generation of about 1330 W/m^2 (Fig. **2**). Mean wind velocities within these areas are 10.61 m/s (Fig. **3**). The direction and frequency of wind occurrence throughout the year are presented in Fig. (**4**) *via* a wind rose diagram.

The prevailing wind patterns at a particular site can be obtained in the form of wind rose diagram, as shown in Fig. (**4**), which is obtained from relevant metrological registration offices, showing information about the distribution of wind velocities as well as the frequency of varying wind directions. For instance, Fig. (**4**) reveals that the east and east–south directions are the directions of prevailing wind patterns for the site in question.

It is worth mentioning that when designing buildings incorporating both solar and wind harvesting technologies, there could be some conflict between the need for south-facing orientation with east or west patterns of wind in the same site, in terms of the orientation of the buildings and opening locations.

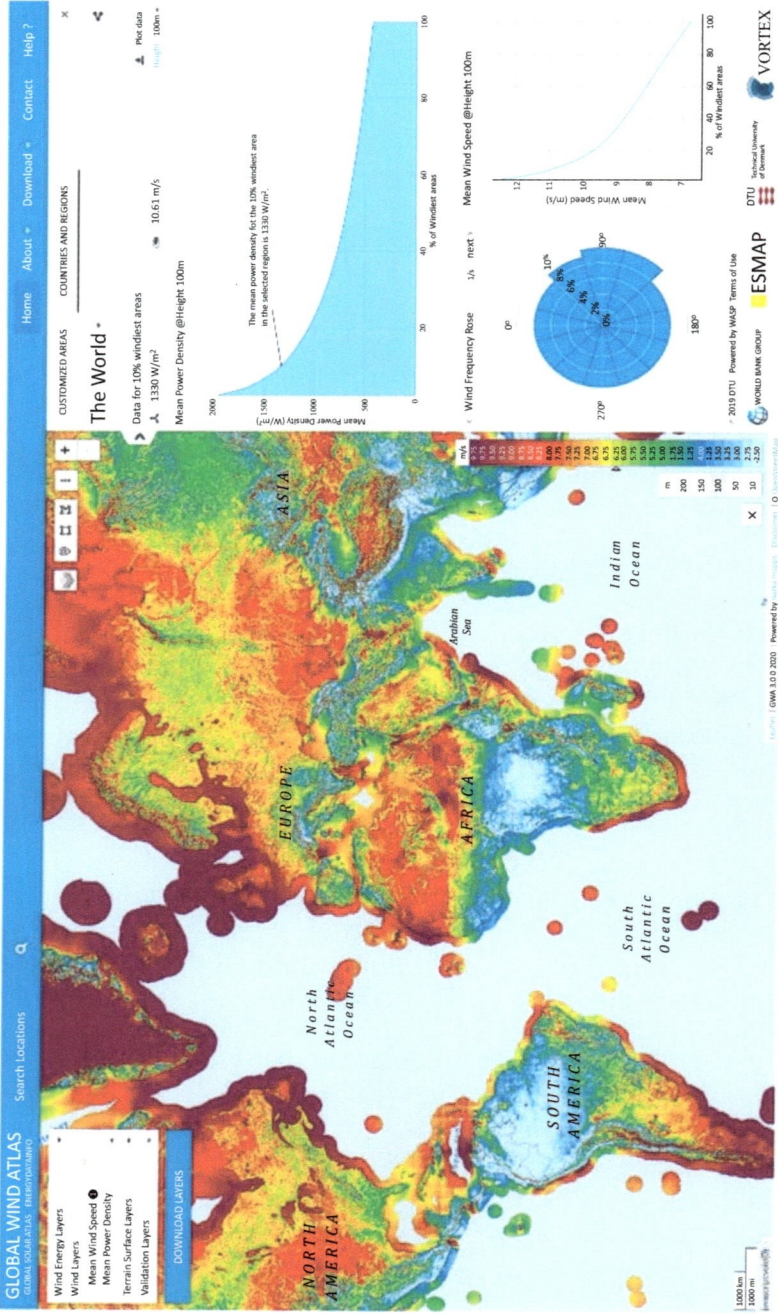

Fig. (1). Global Wind Atlas showing the calculated wind distribution and the likely frequency with micro level details up to 10 × 10 km² at 100 m above ground level [1].

However, for such scenarios, designs for wind energy harvesting will always be more adaptable than those of solar energy harvesting.

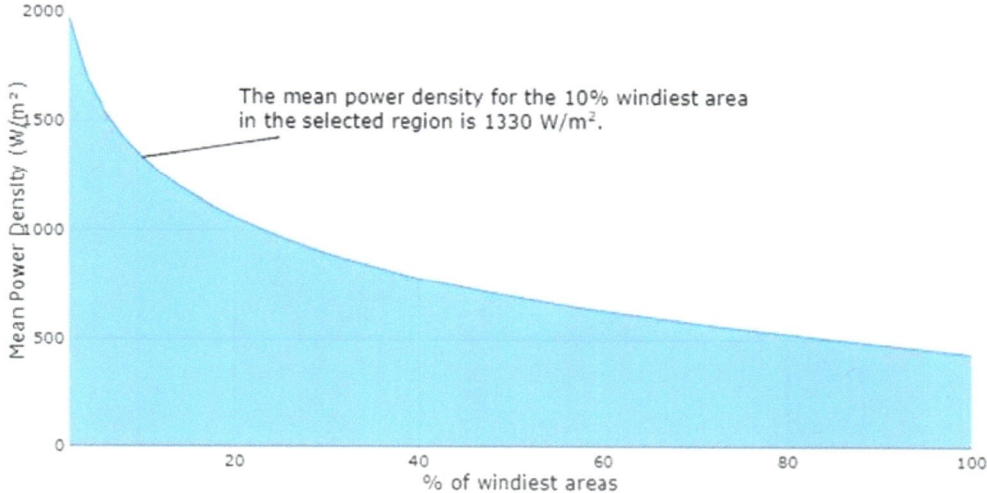

Fig. (2). Area-wise distribution of mean power density, W/m² [1].

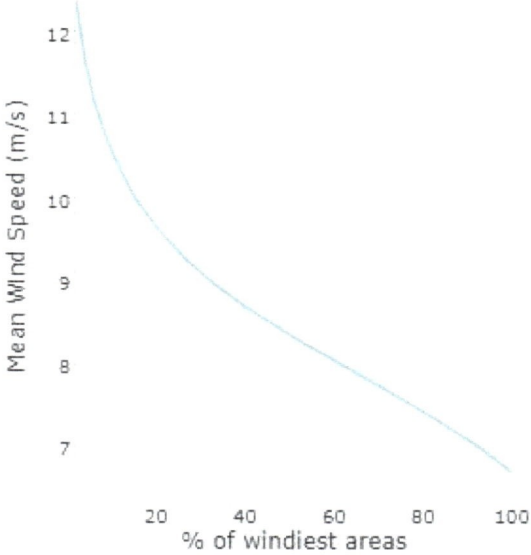

Fig. (3). Area-wise distribution of the mean wind velocities [1].

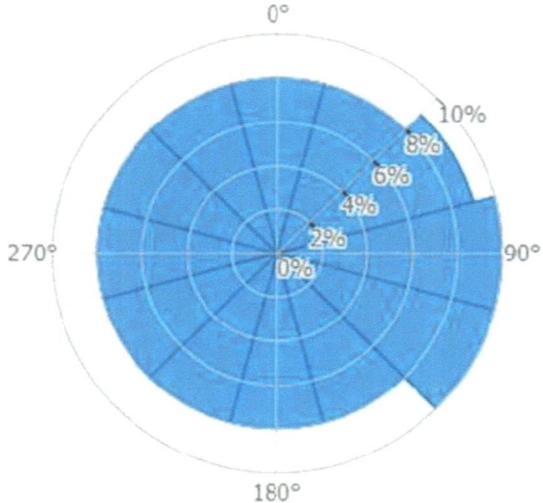

Fig. (4). Wind rose diagram for the direction and frequency of wind occurrence [1].

3. WIND AVAILABILITY WITH HEIGHT

It is a well-established fact that wind energy availability in terms of quantity (*i.e.* wind velocity) and quality (*i.e.* laminar flow, free from turbulence) is greater at higher heights. Figs. (**1, 5, 6 - 8**) show the patterns of wind velocity availability. These figures exhibit the patterns of wind flow at heights of 100 m, 10 m, 50 m, 150 m and 200 m, respectively. The dark red colour represents wind velocities exceeding 10 m/s. The probability of the mean wind velocity increase across the globe extracted from Figs. (**1 – 8**) are presented in Fig. (**9**), wherein a near exponential increase in wind velocity with height is evident. This is further discussed in Chapter 6, section 6.

Fig. (**9**) shows that the beginning of the exponential curve of wind velocities above ground level is in line with the atmospheric boundary layer graphs [6] exhibited in Fig. (**1**), Chapter 2, section 3.1.1. However, due to the limit of height to 200 m above ground level in Fig. (**9**), the full extent of the exponential curve observed in Fig. (**1**), Chapter 2, as it is developed over 50 km above ground level, cannot be seen in Fig. (**9**).

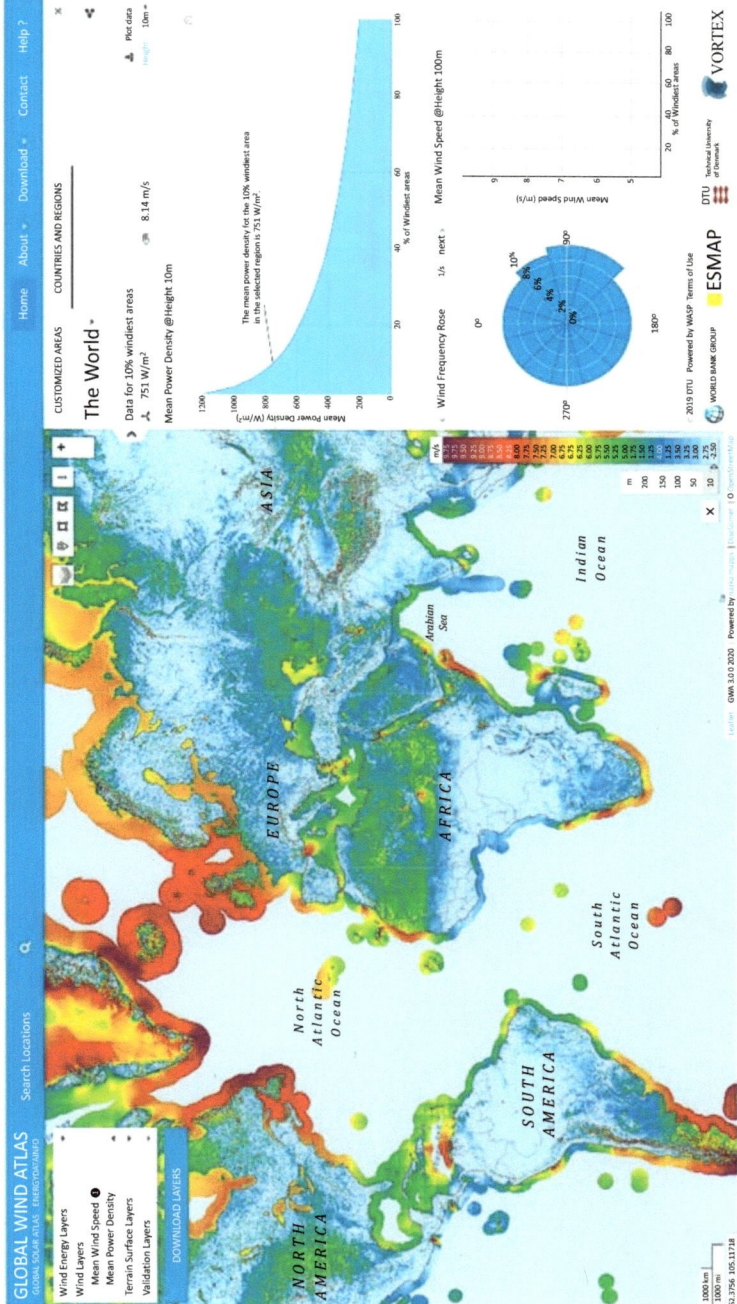

Fig. (5). Global Wind Atlas showing the calculated wind distribution and the likely frequency with micro level details up to 10 × 10 km² at 10 m above ground level [1].

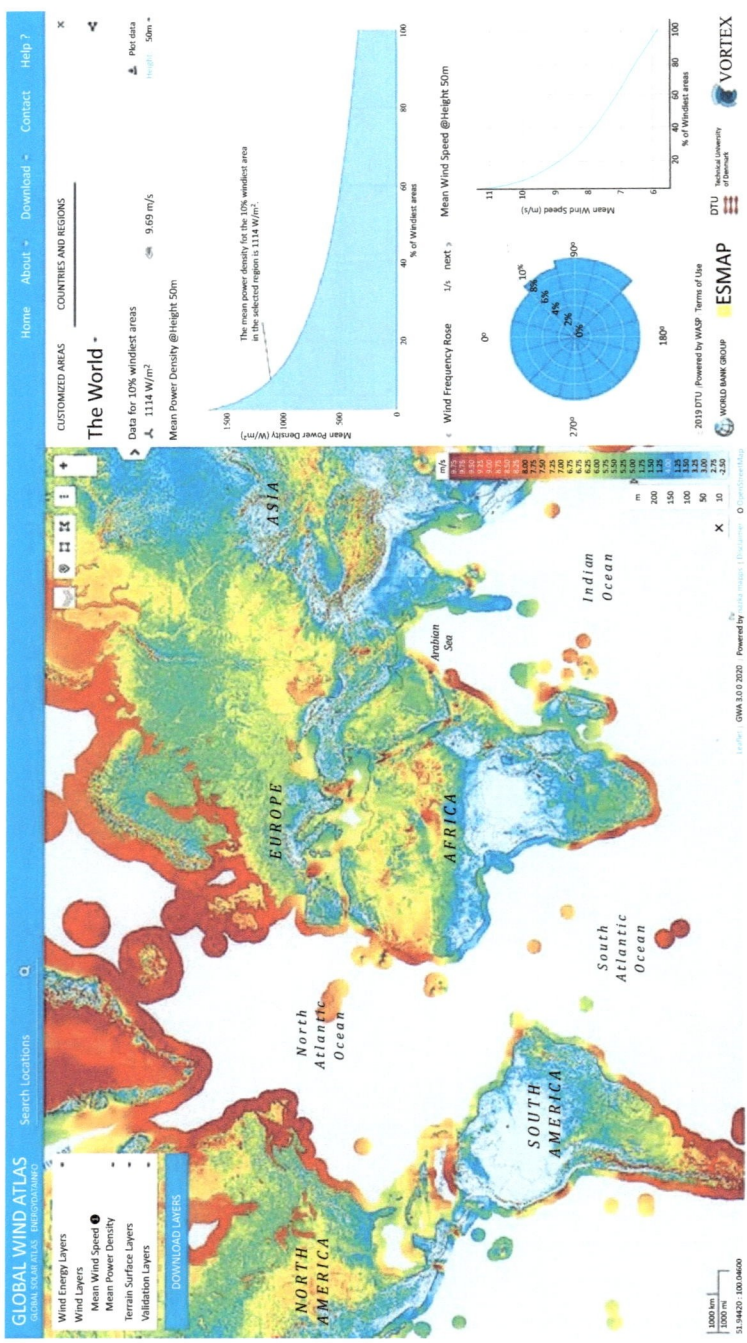

Fig. (6). Global Wind Atlas showing the calculated wind distribution and the likely frequency with micro level details up to 10 × 10 km² at 50 m above ground level [1].

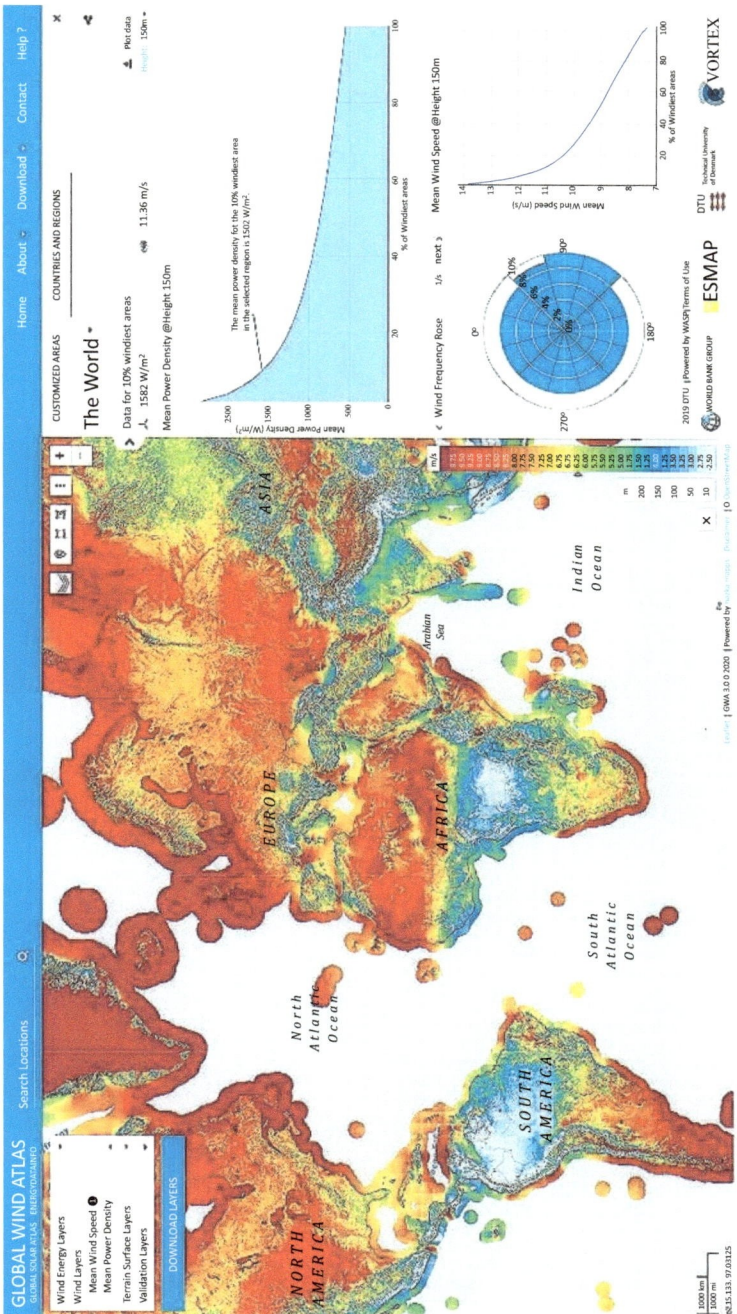

Fig. (7). Global Wind Atlas showing the calculated wind distribution and the likely frequency with micro level details up to 10 × 10 km² at 150 m above ground level [1].

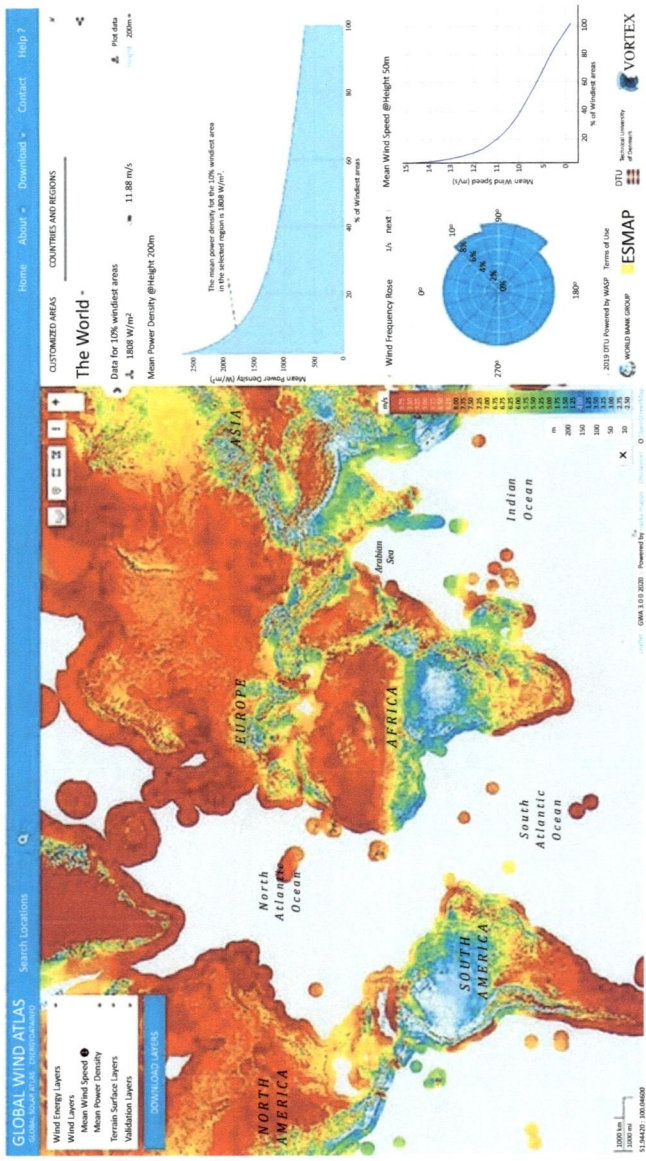

Fig. (8). Global Wind Atlas showing the calculated wind distribution and the likely frequency with micro level details up to 10 × 10 km² at 200 m above ground level [1].

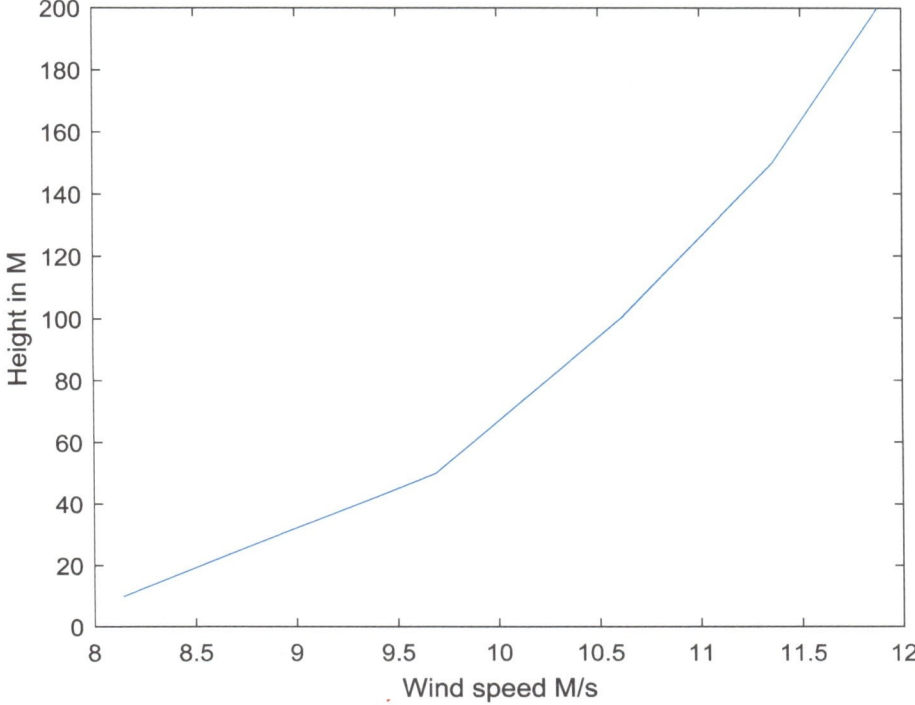

Fig. (9). Distribution of mean wind velocity with height globally.

4. VARIABILITY

Wind energy production can be variable at different time intervals, that is to say the output could vary on hourly, daily, monthly or even yearly basis; however, yearly variations are less critical when compared to the demand.

In general, solar and wind energies tend to complement each other [7]. High-pressure days normally come with clear skies and low wind velocities, maximising possibility for solar energy production. In contrast, low-pressure days are accompanied with cloudy skies and high wind velocities, maximising wind energy potential. Some other innovative solutions to solve this variability of power, voltage and frequency in wind and solar harvesting technologies for example is the Solar Integrated Doubly Fed Induction Generator for Wind Energy Harnessing [8].

5. CAPACITY FACTOR

The capacity factor is the ratio of the actual energy generated using turbines, in a year for instance, to that when turbines are working on full capacity, non-stop for the same period. As mentioned above, wind energy generation is an intermittent process, so eventually, the more interruption to the generation process, the lower the capacity factor will be [9].

The whole idea of having an optimised architectural design for wind energy generation is to reduce this intermittency and provide more consistency in the process. Thus, the capacity factor for any architectural design that incorporates wind energy generation would be a good indicator to the success of that design to generate more power from wind energy. Moreover, it indicates how close an architectural design may be to achieving sustainability.

CONCLUSION

- Wind energy availability can be obtained from metrological data as well as accurately simulated data.
- The height above ground level is a positive factor for producing more power using wind resources.
- Wind energy variability can be resolved by incorporating several backup strategies.
- Capacity factor is a good indicator for the level of improvement an architectural design has to offer, and therefore, it is also a measure of how sustainable the design may be.

REFERENCES

[1] Data/information/map obtained from the Global Wind Atlas 3.0, a. f., web-based application developed, owned and operated by the Technical University of Denmark (DTU). The Global Wind Atlas 3.0 is released in partnership with the World Bank Group, utilizing data provided by Vortex, using funding provided by the Energy Sector Management Assistance Program (ESMAP). For additional information: https://globalwindatlas.info, Data/information/map obtained from the https://globalwindatlas.info

[2] T. Ackermann, "Wind energy technology and current status: a review", *Renew. Sustain. Energy Rev.,* vol. 4, no. 4, pp. 315-374, 2000.
[http://dx.doi.org/10.1016/S1364-0321(00)00004-6]

[3] J. Maldonado, M. Valdiviezo-Condolo, and C. Samaniego, "Wind power forecasting for the villonaco wind farm", *Wind Eng.,* pp. 1-15, 2020.
[http://dx.doi.org/10.1177/0309524X20968817]

[4] M. Ma, B. He, Y. Guan, H. Zhang, and S. Song, "Assessment of global wind energy resource utilization potential, isprs", *Int. Arch. Photogramm. Remote Sens. Spat. Inf. Sci,* vol. XLII-2, no. W7, pp. 1283-1289, 2017.
[http://dx.doi.org/10.5194/isprs-archives-XLII-2-W7-1283-2017]

[5]   M.A. Hyams, "Wind energy in the built environment", In: *Metropolitan Sustainability,* Zeman F., Ed., Woodhead Publishing, 2006, pp. 457-499.

[6]   E. Britannica, *Layers of Earth's atmosphere,* 2020. https://www.britannica.com/science/atmosphere/Troposphere#/media/1/41364/99826

[7]   F. Kaspar, M. Borsche, U. Pfeifroth, J. Trentmann, J. Drücke, and P. Becker, "A climatological assessment of balancing effects and shortfall risks of photovoltaics and wind energy in Germany and Europe", *Advanced Scientific Research,* vol. 16, pp. 119-128, 2019.
[http://dx.doi.org/10.5194/asr-16-119-2019]

[8]   A. Kumar, "Efficient solar integrated doubly fed induction generator for wind energy harnessing", *Recent Adv. Electr. Electron. Eng.,* vol. 13, no. 5, pp. 723-735, 2020.
[http://dx.doi.org/10.2174/2352096512666191019094707]

[9]   Energy, D.O., https://www.energy.gov/ne/articles/what-generation-capacity

CHAPTER 4

Architectural Aerofoil Form Optimisation for Wind Energy Generation

Abstract: This chapter presents a process enabling architectural design to achieve better prospects of integration of wind energy technologies to achieve sustainability. The process aims to utilise architectural forms, masses and profiles to streamline wind flows around buildings for harvesting wind energy using suitable conversion technology (*i.e.* wind turbines). It extends architectural design palette of form-finding rationale in terms of functionality and economic viability forward to achieve sustainability. Computational fluid dynamics (CFD) provided a springboard for navigating, evaluating and optimising design proposals. CFD capability of projecting air movements around buildings considering the magnitude, direction and pressure impact on the building surfaces is of paramount utility. In this chapter, ways and means to utilise wind separation around buildings are examined, together with aerofoil profiles capable of providing conducive conditions for wind flows to be harvested by turbines. Some parameters of these aerofoils are investigated, and guidelines for their optimum performance are defined, namely, aerofoil proximity to the building surface and the angle of attack of the aerofoil. This process would multiply incident wind velocities by up to 30% during periods of low wind velocities (*i.e.* lower than 5 m/s) and up to 150% during periods of high wind velocities (*i.e.* greater than 5 m/s).

Keywords: Aerofoils, Augmented wind energy system, BAWES, CFD, Ducted wind turbine, Fluent, Wind energy optimisation, Wind energy integration in buildings.

1. INTRODUCTION

Wind energy integration into buildings has been gaining growing interest and implementation from both the building industry and the wind energy industry, such as the work of Grant A. and Kelly N. [1], wherein they introduced a prototype of ducted wind turbine at the parapet of a tall building.

The study in this chapter started in 2003 as a part of the author's PhD research that was completed in 2007 [2], was developed further for publication in 2014 [3] and has been updated for this book. Concurrently, since 2007 numerous researchers have worked on small-scale building containing mounted turbines

Abdel Rahman Elbakheit
All rights reserved-© 2021 Bentham Science Publishers

within a shrouded or ducted system. Sharpe T. and Proven G [4]. integrated wind turbines in a concept called Crossflex building. Buildings integrated with vertical-axis wind turbines were worked on by Müller G. *et al* [5]. Suitability and estimation of wind energy generation in urban settings was investigated by Walker S [6]. Buildings integrated with ducted wind turbine prototypes were tested and modelled by Andrew G. *et al* [7]. Site conditions for roof mounted turbines were examined by Ledo L. *et al* [8]. The Makoto Iida proposal of the vernacular design for wind turbines was studied by Chuichi A. and Seiichi A [9].

An innovative design for a ducted wind turbine claiming an extraction power of 80% higher than that of a standalone turbine, nevertheless without building integration, was introduced by Ssu-Yuan H. and Jung-Ho C [10].

A theoretical model and simulation comparison of a ducted wind turbine mounted on a building was introduced by Watson *et al* [11]. The building's influence on wind separation and acceleration and turbine resistance to flow patterns in the duct were discussed by them. They concluded that the inlet of the duct should be optimised in order to improve the swallowing of air into the duct. This is investigated in more detail in sections 6, 7 and 7.1.

Further on the issue of building-integrated wind turbines, this study adopts an approach that focuses on specific scenarios of architectural forms, masses, and components, with favourable conditions suitable for an extra boost to wind energy generation, besides being readily available for replication or reproduction in one way or other. In an attempt to improve the reliability and continuity of wind energy generation, wind separation and its due acceleration is the cornerstone of this investigation. Thus, it is vital to understand how to utilise wind separation in an effective manner.

2. ANALYSIS OF WIND TURBINE INTEGRATION INTO BUILDING DESIGN

2.1. Assumptions

A house with a generic design (Fig. **1**) is prepared to optimise wind energy generation through the integration of wind turbines. Several houses are linked together to form a cluster, which will endorse the assumption of using asymmetry condition for any section across the cluster in CFD simulations.

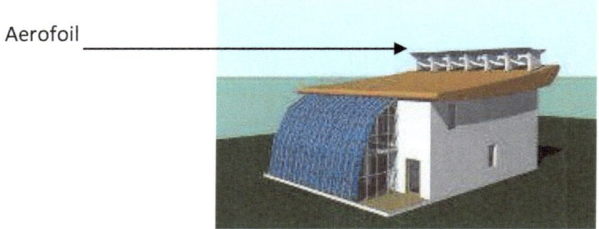

Fig. (1). Typical wind turbine integrated in a prototype house. Aerofoil profile on the high end of the roof.

2.2. Wind Turbine Integration

As mentioned in Chapters 1 and 6, higher heights from the ground level in the built environment would be more suited for integrating wind turbines due to the mainstream flow that is more continuous with less turbulence and interruptions. Therefore, the wind turbines were integrated on top of the roof. The roof is a single-pitch roof sloped to the side facing the wind from the lower edge of the roof. The building façade from windward side shaped like a curved curtain wall starting from the ground and ending at the eave of the roof from its lower edge (Fig. **1**). The curtain-wall façade incorporates photovoltaic panels. However, more importantly, it reduces resistance to wind flow to the top of building where the turbines are placed. An aerofoil is incorporated at the top of the roof with turbines integrated in the space between it and the roof of the house. Vertical-axis wind turbines are fixed with their axes aligned horizontally, as shown in Figs. (**1** and **2**). This allows shorter distances between the aerofoil and the roof to be examined as well as the many benefits of vertical-axis wind turbines, such as quietness, low speed operation and less vibration.

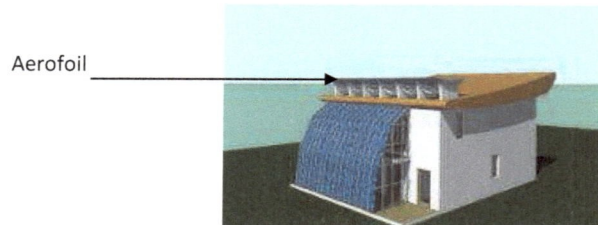

Fig. (2). Typical wind turbine integrated in a prototype house. Aerofoil profile on the low end of the roof.

2.3. Optimising Aerofoil Proximity to Roof Surface

Aerofoil proximity to the roof affects wind velocities and flow pressure. However, in this study, the distance between the aerofoil and the roof is of importance as discussed in section 3.2, mentioned as distance D in Fig. (**10**) in Chapter 2. Another factor comes to play is the shape of the aerofoil, which could either enhance or resist flow and its effect is expressed by the resulting wind velocities.

To examine this proximity to the roof and achieving the optimum distance that produces the maximum resulting wind velocities, a number of distances were studied ranging from 25 to 105 cm. Each distance is subjected to a range of incident wind velocities in CFD simulations. The simulations employed a two-dimensional (2D) unstructured grid for its reliability and speed of calculations. This simulation could be applied to any given design scenario provided that the governing conditions are valid (*i.e.*, boundary conditions). Aspect ratios or building height is discussed in detail in Chapter 6, section 9.

2.4. Underlying Simulation Strategies

Considerable research has been conducted on wind flows in and around built environments since the 1980s. For instance, the blockage effect by buildings has been studied by Oliveira P.J. and Younis B [12]. This blockage affecting the wind flow is particularly important in 2D simulations, necessitating an upstream developing length greater than 15H and a domain height greater than 10H, where H is the height of the obstruction or building, to ensure credibility of domain-independence in CFD simulations. The conditions of the domain were met with, as shown in Fig. (**3**). Oliveira P.J. and Younis B [12]. detailed the accuracy of the expected results using grids of these sizes. The forces acting on the model are gravity, resistances to the flow, the main wind forces and obstructive force due to the aerofoil. For simplification, no heat-related components that can affect to the models were included, *i.e.* no natural convection or convection-related wind movements were considered.

The atmospheric boundary layer was assigned to the computational domain inlet boundary using the standard boundary layer code of the Reynolds stress model (RSM). A ground roughness of 10 mm is assumed for the simulations, as was done by Hoxey and Richard [13].

Generally, for these simulations, 2D grids are preferred over 3D grids as they can describe sections of aerofoil profiles more precisely and easily. Besides, they consume less time in meshing, simulations and convergence as indicated by Oliveira P.J. and Younis B [12]. In addition, no significant reduction in accuracy is reported for the 2D grids compared to the 3D grids.

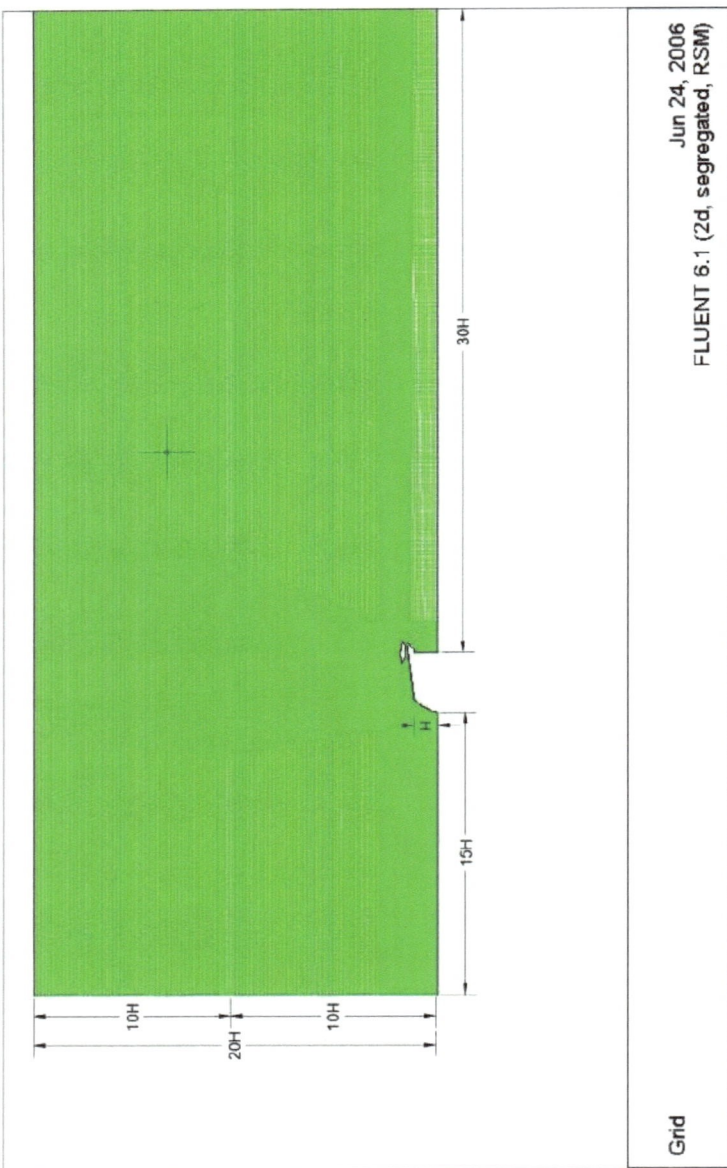

Fig. (3). 2D mesh for the case of an 85-cm distance between the aerofoil and the roof.

2.5. Computational Fluid Dynamics

The computational technology that equips researchers with tools to examine fluids dynamics is CFD. Through CFD, researchers can build a virtual model of the domain (*i.e.* grid) of a device or system under study. The software solves mass, momentum and energy conservation equations, such as the Navier–Stokes equations [14], after the researchers enter the applicable fluid flow parameters and the boundary conditions into the virtual model. The outputs are portrayed as predictions of the flow parameters in terms of flow velocity, direction, pressure, temperature, *etc.*, within the specified domain.

In the present investigation, k-ε model and RSM were used to solve for air flow velocity magnitudes and direction as well as patterns of air movements. The standard k-ε is expressed as follows:

Turbulent kinetic energy, k: =

$$\underbrace{\mu_t \left(\frac{\partial U_j}{\partial x_i} + \frac{\partial U_i}{\partial x_j} \right) \frac{\partial U_j}{\partial x_i}}_{generation} + \underbrace{\frac{\partial}{\partial x_i}\left[\frac{\mu_t \partial k}{\sigma_k \partial x_i} \right]}_{diffusion} - \underbrace{\rho \varepsilon}_{dissipation} \qquad (1)$$

Dissipation rate, ε=

$$\underbrace{C_{1\varepsilon}\left(\frac{\varepsilon}{k}\right)\mu_t \left(\frac{\partial U_j}{\partial x_i} + \frac{\partial U_i}{\partial x_j} \right) \frac{\partial U_j}{\partial x_i}}_{generation} + \underbrace{\frac{\partial}{\partial x_i}\left[\frac{\mu_t}{\sigma_\varepsilon} \frac{\partial \varepsilon}{\partial x_i} \right]}_{diffusion} - \underbrace{C_{2\varepsilon}\rho\left(\frac{\varepsilon}{k}\right)}_{destruction} \qquad (2)$$

where ρ is the fluid density, U_ and x_ denote the velocity component and coordinate, respectively.

The RSM can be simplified as follows:

$$\frac{\partial u_i}{\partial t} + u_j \frac{\partial u_i}{\partial x_j} = \frac{\partial p}{\partial x_i} + v\nabla^2 u_i \qquad (3)$$

$$\frac{\partial u_i}{\partial x_j} = 0 \qquad (4)$$

where u_i is the velocity vector, p is the modified pressure (may contain a gravitational component), and v is the kinematic viscosity of the fluid. In (3) and (4), the Einstein summation convention applies to the repeated indices.

2.5.1. Effect of Domain Size

As discussed in section 2.4, the domain size of the simulation has to be within a specific size to guarantee the plausibility of the obtained results of changes in air flow magnitude and nature because of the change in the proximity of the aerofoil to the roof. The recommended domain size is revealed in Fig. (**3**).

2.5.2. Mesh-independent Solution

High precision of the mesh with special treatment to the points of junctions, the bottom side of the aerofoil and the upper side of the roof was employed. Mesh refinement for the windward and leeward sides are presented in Fig. (**4**) [15].

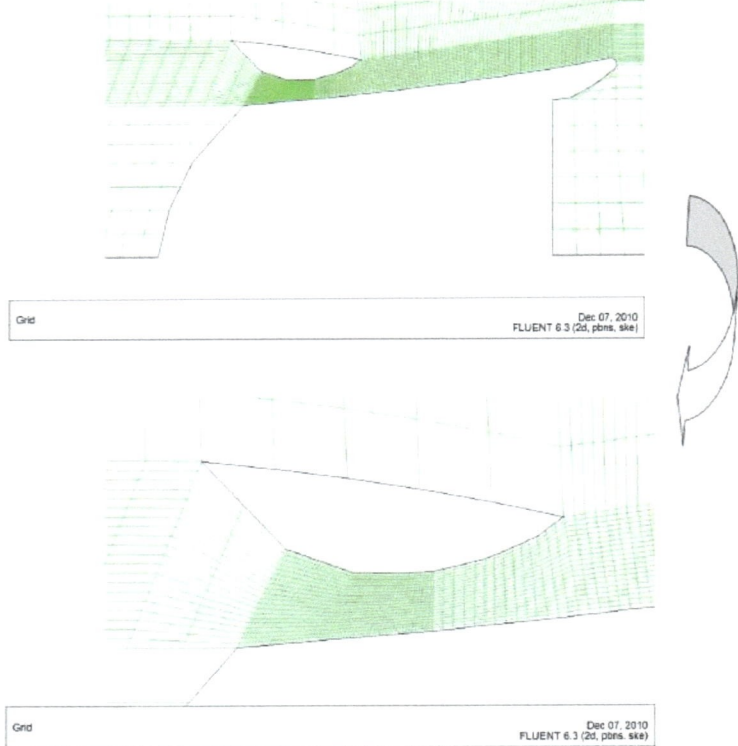

Fig. (4). Mesh refinement and adaptation of the underside of the aerofoil and the upper side of the roof and façade.

Special care is exerted for obtaining solution accuracy *via* the selection of the cell types, adaptation to the mesh in addition to the former treatment to the mesh. Hexagonal cells, with an aspect ratio near one, are employed due to their high accuracy and low skewness, especially in areas below the aerofoil. Mesh adaptations keeps the Y+ distance within the boundary layer. (Y+ is the viscous length, a non-dimensional perpendicular length from bounding wall). This should model the attachment and separation of the wind accurately and without too lengthy calculations. In addition to the previous mesh size guidelines and as a second proof of grid credibility and its results, a mesh independence verification study is conducted. Here, six mesh sizes (Table 1) are investigated to determine the resulting velocities lower than the aerofoil with inlet velocity of 4.2 m/s; this situation is similar to that in a practical experiment conducted by Grassmann *et al* [16]; consult Table 1 of Grassmann *et al* (*i.e.* a 4.2 m/s incident wind velocity yielded 7.95 m/s when using a shrouded turbine).

Table 1. Mesh sizes tested under an incident wind velocity of 4.2 m/s to determine their impact on the results.

Grid	Number of Cells	Inlet Velocity m/s	Y+	Predicted Velocity m/s	Deviation from the Experimental Yield [16]
1	22,906	4.2	53	5.97	−24.90%
2	45,147	4.2	52	6.90	−13.2%
3	46,326	4.2	29.9	8.06	+1.38%
4	53,290	4.2	21	8	+0.63%
5	54,832	4.2	12.6	8.10	+1.88%
6	66,811	4.2	0.10	7.88	+0.88%

From Table 1 in this chapter, we can conclude that with mesh size increases from 53.290 cells and higher, marginal deviation of the grid results experienced from that of the above-mentioned experimental results. This ascertains that the grid attained independence from mesh size from 53.290 cells onwards.

2.5.3. Grid Convergence Study

To measure the grid convergence, Roaches' grid convergence study is conducted. The positive results reinforce confidence in the results obtained by the selected grid. Roaches' [17] grid convergence index GDI_{25} gives an error range on the grid convergence. The GDI can best be calculated at three levels to accurately estimate the order of convergence and to check that the solutions are within the asymptotic range of convergence.

The first step in the GDI study, according to Roaches, is to determine the order of convergence observed for the predicted velocities in Table **1**, grids 6 and 5, as follows:

$$\text{The order } (p) = \ln\left[(7.88 - 8.10) / (8.10 - 8)\right] / \ln(2) = 1.1375 \tag{5}$$

The second step is to apply the Richardson extrapolation for grids 4 and 5 in Table 1, followed by the same for grids 5 and 6,

$$GDI_{45} = 1.25 \,|\, (8 - 8.1) / 8 \,|\, / (2^{1.137504} - 1)\, 100\% = 1.302083\% \tag{6}$$

$$GDI_{56} = 1.25 \,|\, (8.1 - 7.88) / 8.1 \,|\, / (2^{1.137504} - 1)\, 100\% = 2.829216\% \tag{7}$$

Now, we can check whether the solutions are within asymptotic range of convergence.

$$2.829216 / (2^{1.137504}\, 1.302083) = 0.98765351 \tag{8}$$

This value, 0.98765351, which is very close to one, indicates that the solutions of these three grids are well within the asymptotic range of convergence.

Applying the same GDI procedure for grids 1, 2 and 3 yields an accuracy of 0.863768. This emphasises that the solution would be mesh independent from a mesh of 53,290 cells and larger grids, and grid 53,290 can be confirmed to be sufficient for obtaining plausible results for the simulation.

2.6. The Effect of Models of Turbulence

The cases represented the study on aerofoil and building under atmospheric boundary conditions can be completely categorised as turbulent models of discretisation. This is because the calculated Re for it is 6×10^6, which is obtained using the characteristic length of 6 m, which is the length of the aerofoil. The reason behind using such a large aerofoil is to further streamline the flow and to reduce any resulting turbulence from the front of the building within the area under the aerofoil. The length of 6 m is not regarded as large, considering the size of typical buildings.

To obtain a general overview of the effect of the different turbulence models available for these cases, both the k-ε model and RSM are applied to the above verified grids. The resulting wind flow patterns and velocities under the aerofoil are presented in Figs. (**5** and **6**). These figures show that the k-ε model did not sufficiently describe the area or recirculation next to the top of the roof and in front of the aerofoil, which was portrayed by the RSM.

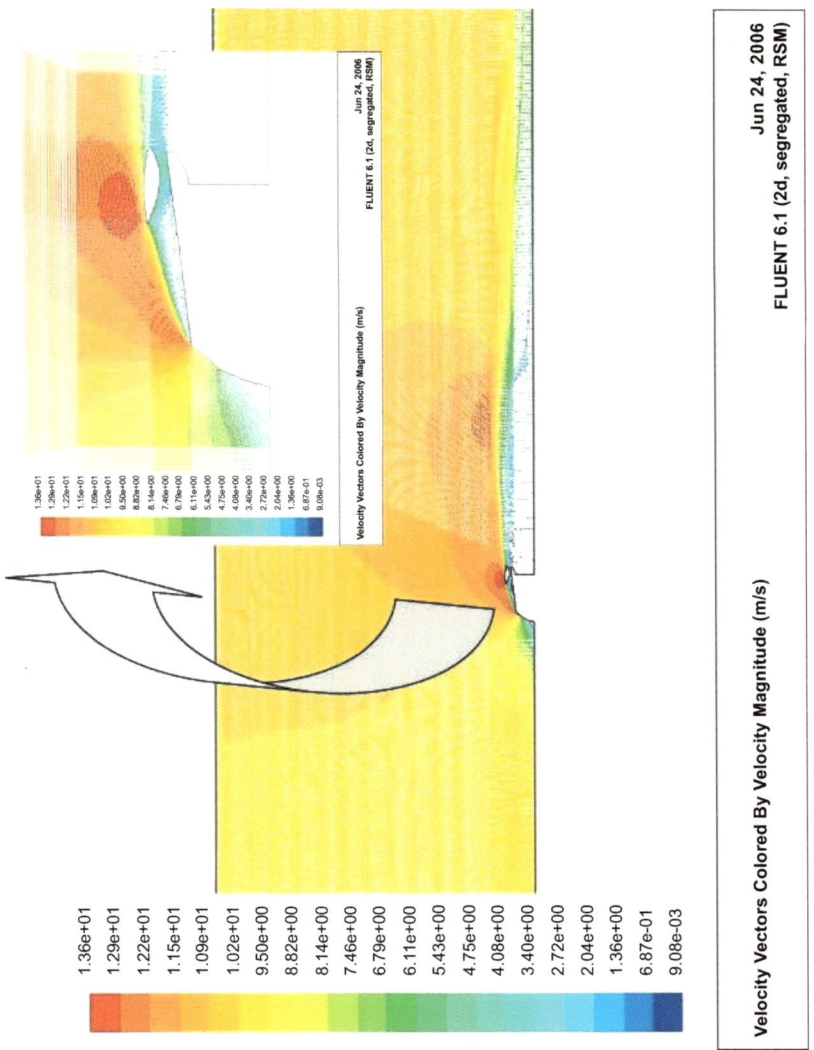

Fig. (5). Resulting velocity vectors for the case of an 85cm distance between the wing and the rooftop (Reynolds Stress Model).

Despite the fact that the incident wind velocities into the inlet for the cases in Figs. (**5** and **6**) are different, both the RSM and k-ε model had similar resulting velocities when using any set of unified boundary conditions, which are same as those found by Hoxey and Richards [11] and Hoxey *et al* [12]. This makes the RSM better suited for the undertaken simulations of the effect of the proximity of the aerofoil to the roof.

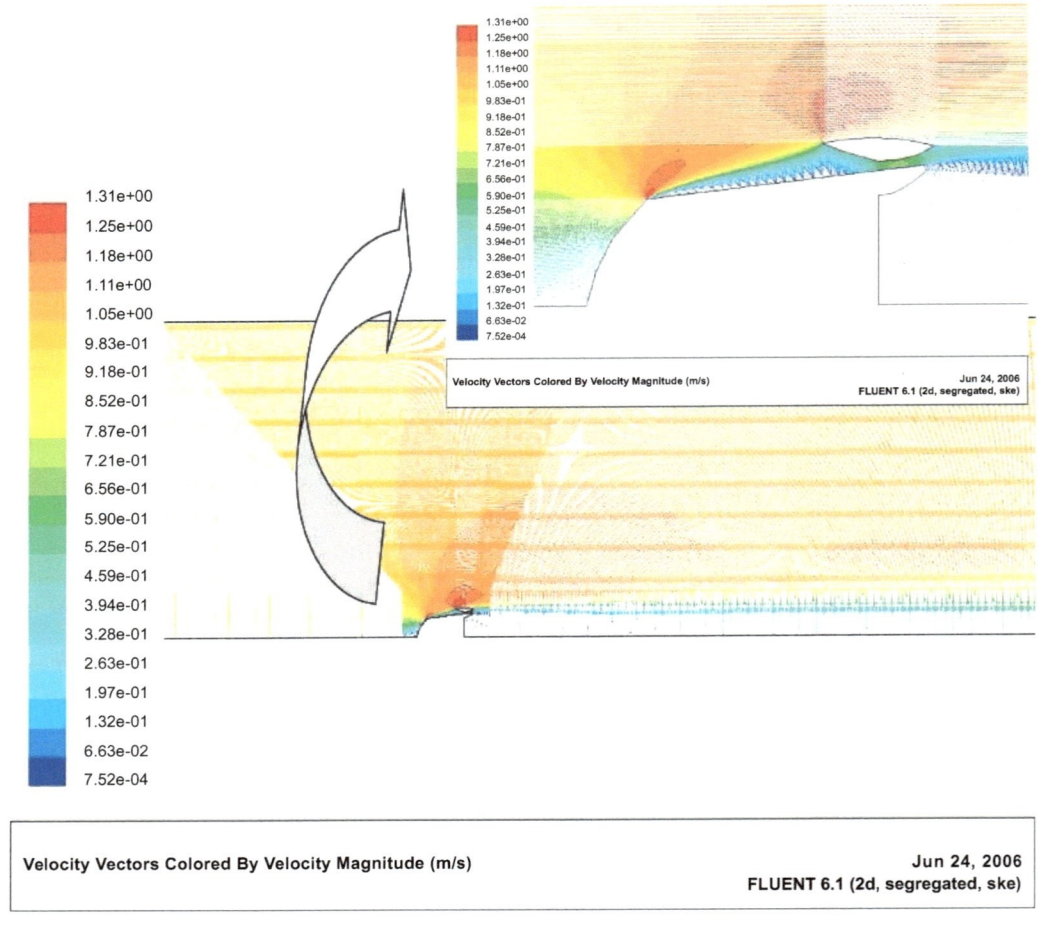

Fig. (6). The resulting velocity vectors for the case of an 85-cm distance between the aerofoil and the roof (k-ε model).

To assess the difference between the resulting velocities obtained from the two models, these models were applied on a single case one at a time with all other factors and boundary conditions being identical. The result is presented in Table 2.

Table 2. Comparison of the predicted velocities by the RSM and the k-ε models.

Turbulence Model	Inlet of 1 m/s	Inlet of 2 m/s	Inlet of 3 m/s	Inlet of 4 m/s	Inlet of 5 m/s	Inlet of 6 m/s	Inlet of 7 m/s	Inlet of 8 m/s	Inlet of 9 m/s	Inlet of 10 m/s
k-ε	1.52	3.4	5.15	6.9	8.7	10.4	11.8	13.9	15.7	17.4
RSM	1.83	3.7	5.6	7.6	9.5	11.4	13.2	15.2	17.1	19

From Table 2, we can deduce that the RSM predicts resulting velocities 10% higher than those predicted by the k-ε model for all ten examined incident wind velocities, except for the incident wind velocity of 1 m/s, for which the prediction was 25% higher. This result for the 1 m/s incident wind velocity would not be of significant importance, considering the anticipated power generation from wind can only be obtained from higher incident wind velocities.

However, for the other parameter that affects wind flow patterns around the aerofoil and the building, *i.e.* the angle of attack, the situation is a bit different. This is because the RSM consumes more time for full convergence, but it produces a solution quite similar to that obtained by the k-ε model. Therefore, for the angle of attack, the k-ε model was used instead in section 5.1 to save time.

While the model solutions provided a good comparison of the flow around the aerofoil and the building, it also revealed that the anticipated upper location of the aerofoil at the highest point of the roof actually produced double separation of the flow. The first separation was at the eave and the second separation at the tip of the aerofoil, with lower resulting velocities between the aerofoil and the roof. Therefore, to eliminate the second separation, we can relocate the aerofoil over the eave.

2.7. The Effect of the Aerofoil Position on Top of the Roof

The investigation of the flow in section 2.6 revealed the loss of wind momentum and the production of multiple separations that would lead to additional turbulences and recirculations all over the domain. To reduce turbulence and further enhance wind flow streamlining, the aerofoil can be relocated to the area above the eave of the building. Hence, we have two new cases that need to be compared, the aerofoil above the peak of the roof and the aerofoil above the eave, as shown in Figs. (**5** and **7**), respectively. The two cases share identical parameters of the domain, incident wind velocities and turbulence model (*i.e.* RSM). Moreover, they both are run under incident wind velocity of 10 m/s.

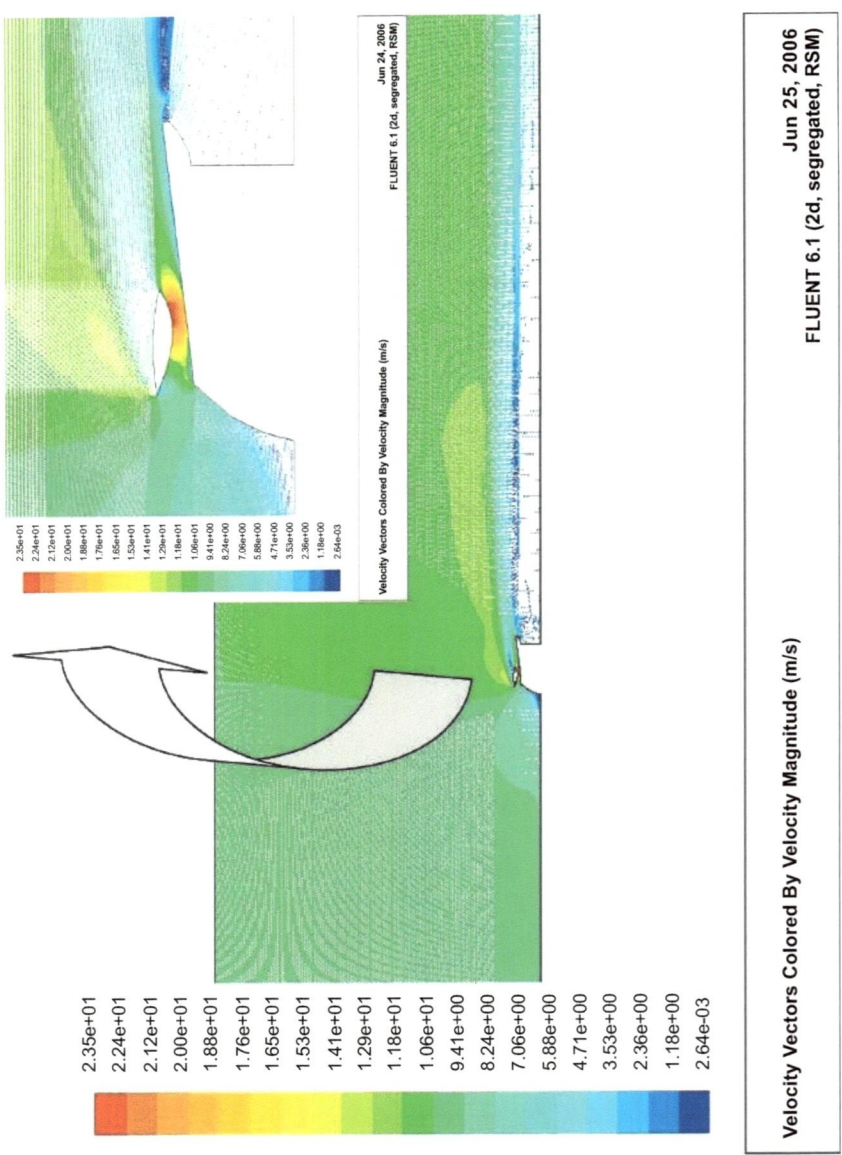

Fig. (7). Velocity vectors for the aerofoil placed above the eave at the front of the house.

When examining the results of Figs.(**5** and **7**), we can see that shifting the aerofoil over the eave reduces turbulence over the entire domain with recirculation above and beyond the aerofoil and a small area from the front of the house, as shown in Fig. (**7**). However, the acceleration effect only existed below the aerofoil and not in the entire domain, as shown in Fig. (**5**).

As for the resulting wind velocities, the aerofoil above the eave produced a maximum velocity of 23.53 m/s, while the aerofoil above the peak of the roof produced a maximum velocity of 4.75 m/s. This proves that placing aerofoil above the eave is four-times more successful than placing it above the peak of the roof.

2.8. The Effect of Different Wind Directions

Further, to study the different aerofoil positions, we can investigate the effect of changing the wind direction, where the windward side becomes the leeward side or vice versa. In reality, details of wind velocities and directions can be obtained from the wind rose diagram, which shows the directions and magnitudes of wind from all directions. The opposite direction wind flows normally alternate between summer and winter for example. In this situation, a 2D grid provides a major benefit to simulate opposing wind direction. Therefore, the same two cases of aerofoil positions above the eave and above the peak of the roof discussed in section 2.7 are run using RSM to examine the resulting wind velocities under the aerofoil.

Here, we consider that the main direction of wind from left to right is the primary or major wind direction, whereas wind direction from right to left is the secondary or minor direction. The results of running the cases as mentioned are presented in Tables **3** and **4**, respectively.

Table 3. Effect of the wind direction from the left side of the building (primary).

Direction of the Wind	Resulting Velocity Below the Aerofoil in m/s
Front wind (from left)	23.53
Back wind	3.5

Table 4. Effect of the wind direction from the right side of the building (secondary).

Direction of the Wind	Resulting Velocity Below the Aerofoil in m/s
Front wind (from right)	4.75
Back wind	14.3

Tables **3** and **4** reveal that when wind is approaching the two cases of aerofoil positions, *i.e.* above the eave and top of the roof peak, the former position scored the obtained maximum resulting velocity of 23.53 m/s under the aerofoil, whereas the latter performed better by achieving resulting velocities under the aerofoil of 14.3 m/s, when it is subjected to wind from the right side of the domain.

From this investigation, we can conclude that placing the aerofoil above the eave of the house would be the most successful. However, in practical terms, the final choice of aerofoil position may rest on the statistics of wind directions, magnitudes and occurrences over the years based on a wind rose diagram of the site in question. This is to achieve the maximum possible yearly wind energy generation.

2.9. Summary of Optimising the Aerofoil Proximity to the Roof of the House

Aerofoil proximity to the roof is optimised by employing the case with the aerofoil placed above the roof, as discussed in section 2.7, because it produced the maximum velocity under the aerofoil. The optimisation involved subjecting the aerofoil with 10 consecutive incident wind velocities across the aerofoil while varying aerofoil distance from the roof. These distances were varied from 60 cm to 105 cm (*i.e.*, refered to as widths' in Figs. (**8** and **9**).

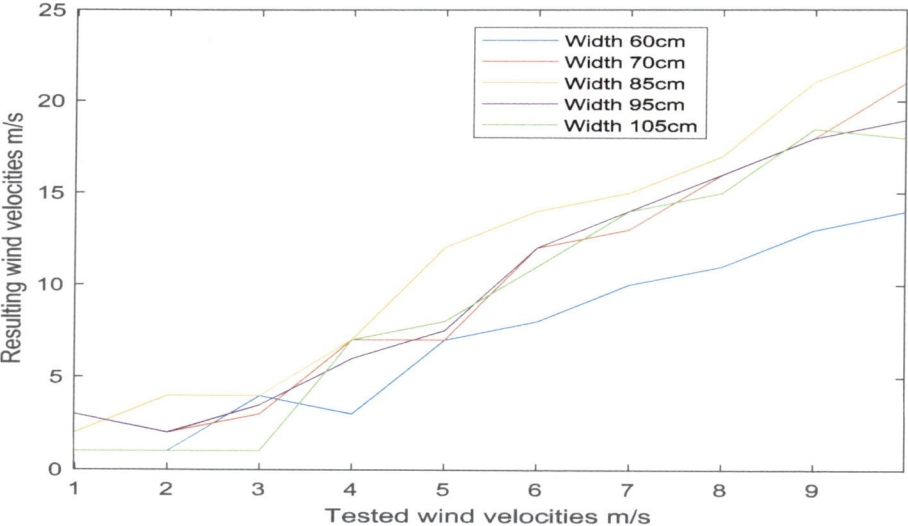

Fig. (8). Comparison of the resulting velocities based on the examined widths at various tested velocities. (in series).

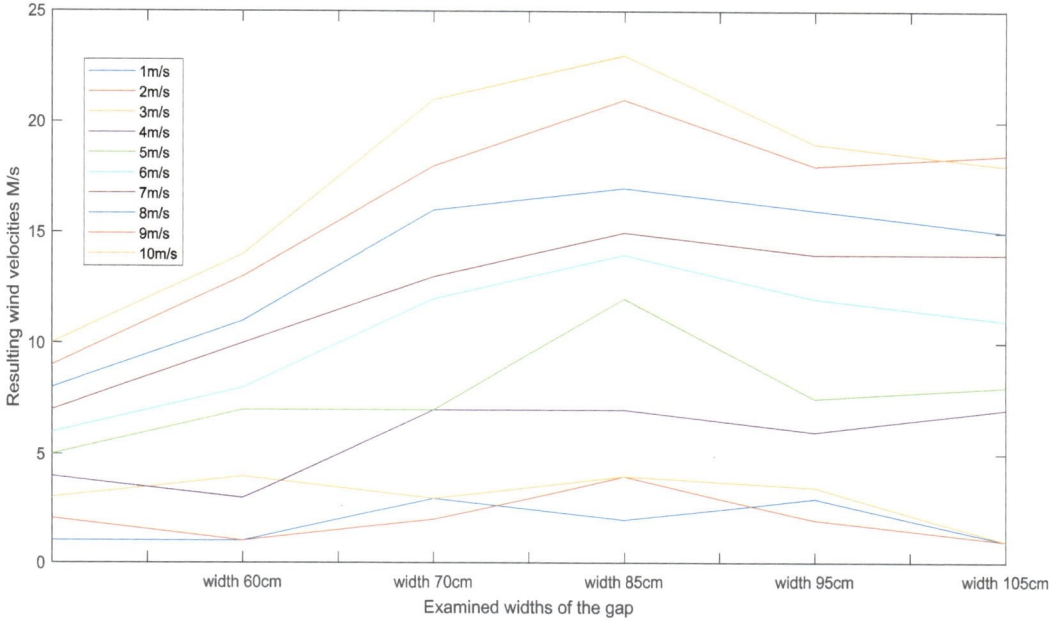

Fig. (9). Comparison of the resulting velocities based on the examined widths at various tested velocities.

According to these figures the resulting wind velocities under the aerofoil increased with increasing distance between the aerofoil and the roof from 60 cm to 85 cm (achieved at just below 25 m/s), while a gradual decline in the resulting velocities is evident beyond 85-cm distance. Therefore, the distance of 85 cm of the aerofoil from the roof is the optimum distance in this case.

2.10. Summary of Optimisation of the Aerofoil Front Shape

The aerofoil front shape is optimised by increasing the angle of attack of the aerofoil to introduce more mass flow rate between the aerofoil and the roof. The angle of attack is gradually increased presented in Fig. (**10**). The reason for the low incremental step is the fact that they produced larger separations of flow, which reduces the resulting velocities, as revealed in Fig. (**11**).

Since the optimum distance between the aerofoil and the roof is determined to be 85 cm, using this distance to maintain the highest resulting wind velocity is a priority. Therefore, opening the entrance of the aerofoil further is what is required to introduce higher mass flow. This made the definition of angle of attack in general aerodynamics as 'the angle between direction of flow and centre line of profile' slightly different than the opening angle description in this optimisation (Fig. **10**).

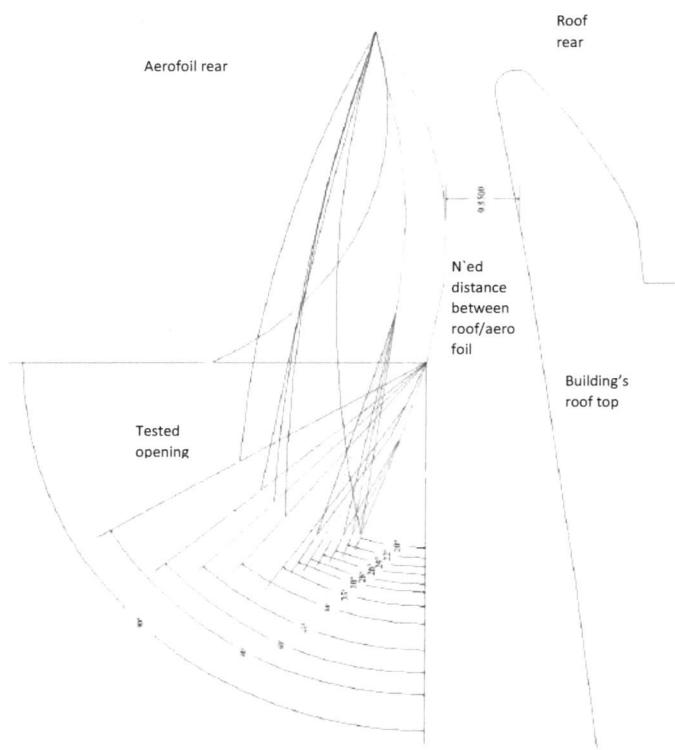

Fig. (10). Schematic showing the different angles of attack of the aerofoils.

2.11. Effect of Increasing the Angle of Attack

This section elaborates on the discussion in sections 2 and 5 on increasing the angle of attack to allow more wind under the aerofoil. The investigation of this parameter consumed more time in obtaining convergence using the RSM. Therefore, the study can be simplified by employing the k-ε model with little loss of accuracy, as presented in section 2.6. Therefore, the study on angle of attack used 10 consecutive incident wind velocities to the domain for cases of angles of attack increasing systematically using the k-ε model.

After CFD simulations of the cases with incremental increase in angle of attack by 2° intervals, high-intensity turbulence and recirculation were present that produced a reduction in the resulting velocities, which is experienced with the increase in angle of attack from angles 20° to 30°. However, an increase in the resulting velocities is reported for angles ranging from 40° to 50° (Fig. **11**). However, further increase in angle of attack beyond 50° produced lower resulting velocities under the aerofoil. This proves that the angle of 50° is the optimum angle of attack for this aerofoil shape. It worth mentioning that the 10 consecutive incident wind velocities all presented the same profile of increase in resulting velocities over the entire studied range of angles (Fig. **11**). This also further reinforces the fact that angle of 50° is the optimum angle of attack.

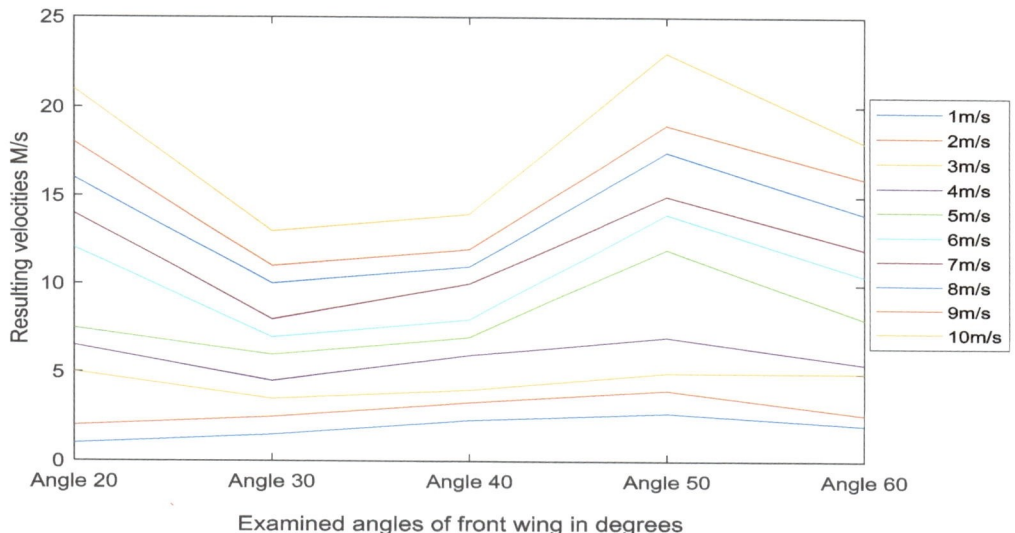

Fig. (11). Comparison of the resulting velocities based on optimized width of 85cm at various tested velocities and angles of attack.

3. POWER ESTIMATION

The wind power can be expressed as follows:

$$P_w = 0.5 \rho A v^3 \qquad (9)$$

where ρ is the air density, Kg/m³, A is the cross-sectional area, m², and V is the air velocity, m/s.

This equation certifies the importance of wind velocity in determining the power generation from wind. Nevertheless, various wind turbine designs have different energy conversion efficiencies and resistance to flow. However, despite these factors, the design of the aerofoil considered in this study accelerates wind in excess of the Betz limit (*i.e.* 59.3%) as proven by H. Grassmann *et al* [15]. Grassmann suggested that acceleration due to aerofoil equals the ratio between V3, which is the velocity under the aerofoil, and two-thirds of V0, which is the wind velocity far in front of the aerofoil. When conducting this ratio on the results provided by CFD FLUENT simulations in Tables C and D, as described in section 2.8, we obtain ratios of 0.53, 0.71, 2.15 and 3.5 for the resulting velocities of 3.5 m/s, 4.75 m/s, 14.3 m/s and 23.5 m/s, respectively. This shows that the Betz Limit exceeded three out of four times. In addition, this reinforces the significance of both the positioning and parameters of the depicted aerofoil profile.

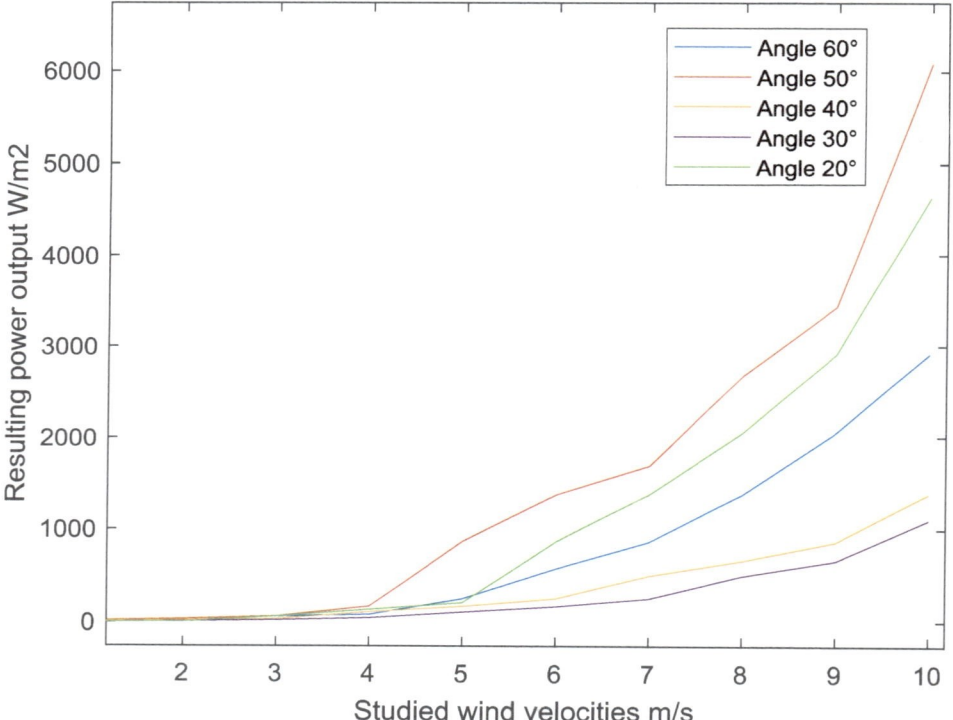

Fig. (12). Resulting power output at different wind velocities and angles of attack.

3.1. Effect of Aerofoil Angle of Attack and Aerofoil Proximity on the Power Output

Estimations of power generation outcome due to the optimisations of the angles of attack and proximities of the aerofoil to the roof provides a clear picture of the usefulness of these optimisation to the power outcome. Since power mainly depends on wind velocities in the power equation (9), the resulting velocities from the optimisation would provide estimations of power generation and therefore indicate the usefulness of the optimisations that produced these velocities. Figs. (**12** and **13**) show the power generation estimation from the resulting velocities in the optimisation of the area under the aerofoil. Fig. (**12**) shows that the power yield of angle of attack of 30° is lower than that of the angle of attack of 20°. However, the power yield consecutively improves as the angle of attack changes from 30° to 40° and 50°. The power yield from 60° is lower than that from 50°. Hence, 50° is the optimum angle of attack for this aerofoil shape. Fig. (**13**) shows the incremental power improvement for each studied angle of attack, wherein the angle of 50° provided the only consistent power improvement; nevertheless, this consistency is more pronounced for incident wind velocities of 5 m/s and greater.

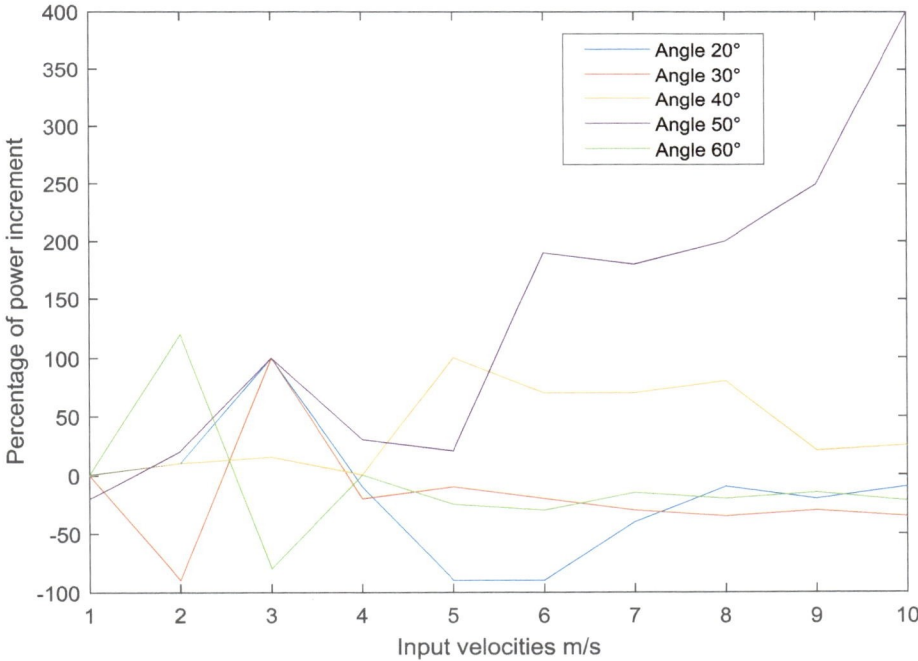

Fig. (13). Percentage of power increment as the angle of attack increases.

CONCLUSION

The following conclusions can be drawn from the study:

- CFD assists in examining the flow conditions around buildings and guiding the optimisation wind flows for optimum performance of wind energy technologies.

- The study has confirmed the usefulness of aerofoils in augmenting wind flows that would be harvested using turbines with efficiencies exceeding the Betz limit compared to those of standalone turbines.
- The investigated aerofoil profile could accelerate wind velocities by factors varying from 0.53 to 3.5 folds, compared to Betz limit that is from below the limit to over six fold of the limit, depending on present wind flows.
- Aerofoils to boost wind energy can be incorporated into buildings during design or after construction. Small- to medium-sized Savonious vertical-axis wind turbines are recommended for use with aerofoils.
- Main factors influencing wind acceleration by using aerofoils is the proximity of the aerofoil from the building surfaces and the angles of attack.
- This investigation revealed that an angle of attack of 50° would assist the aerofoil in question to achieve the highest possible wind acceleration.
- The proximity of the aerofoil to the roof of the building that delivered best possible wind acceleration 85 cm.
- This investigation has shown that aerofoil position has a great influence on the ensued wind acceleration owing to the aerofoil, which together with careful planning for wind separation secures successful performance.
- This process can be applied to any given building design to guarantee optimum performance.

REFERENCES

[1] A.D. Grant, C.M. Johnstone, and N. Kelly, *Urban wind energy conversion*, 2007.

[2] A.R. Elbakheit, Enhanced architectural integration of photovoltaics and wind turbines into building Design., 2007.

[3] A.R. Elbakheit, "Factors enhancing aerofoil wings for wind energy harnessing in buildings", *Build. Serv. Eng. Res. Tech.*, vol. 35, no. 4, pp. 417-437, 2014.
[http://dx.doi.org/10.1177/0143624413509097]

[4] T. Sharpe, and G. Proven, "Crossflex: Concept and early development of a true building integrated wind turbine", *Energy Build.*, vol. 42, no. 12, pp. 2365-2375, 2010.
[http://dx.doi.org/10.1016/j.enbuild.2010.07.032]

[5] G. Müller, M.F. Jentsch, and E. Stoddart, "Vertical axis resistance type wind turbines for use in buildings", *Renew. Energy*, vol. 34, no. 5, pp. 1407-1412, 2009.
[http://dx.doi.org/10.1016/j.renene.2008.10.008]

[6] S.L. Walker, "Building mounted wind turbines and their suitability for the urban scale—A review of methods of estimating urban wind resource", *Original Research Article, Energy and Buildings*, vol. 43, no. 8, pp. 1852-1862, 2011.
[http://dx.doi.org/10.1016/j.enbuild.2011.03.032]

[7] G. Andrew, J. Cameron, and K. Nick, "Urban wind energy conversion: The potential of ducted turbines", *Renew. Energy*, vol. 33, no. 6, pp. 1157-1163, 2008.
[http://dx.doi.org/10.1016/j.renene.2007.08.005]

[8] L. Ledo, P.B. Kosasih, and P. Cooper, "Roof mounting site analysis for micro-wind turbines", *Renew. Energy*, vol. 36, no. 5, pp. 1379-1391, 2011.
[http://dx.doi.org/10.1016/j.renene.2010.10.030]

[9] A. Chuichi, A. Seiichi, and L. Makoto, "Proposal of vernacular design for wind turbine", *J. Wind Eng. Ind. Aerodyn.,* vol. 90, no. 12-15, pp. 1731-1741, 2002.
[http://dx.doi.org/10.1016/S0167-6105(02)00283-0]

[10] S.Y. Hu, and J.H. Cheng, "Innovatory designs for ducted wind turbines", *Renew. Energy,* vol. 33, no. 7, pp. 1491-1498, 2008.
[http://dx.doi.org/10.1016/j.renene.2007.08.009]

[11] S.J. Watson, D.G. Infield, J.P. Barton, and S.J. Wylie, "Modelling of the performance of a building-mounted ducted wind turbine", *J. Phys. Conf. Ser.,* vol. 75, p. 012001, 2007.
[http://dx.doi.org/10.1088/1742-6596/75/1/012001]

[12] P.J. Oliveira, and B.A. Younis, "On the prediction of turbulent flows around full-scale buildings", *J. Wind Eng. Ind. Aerodyn.,* vol. 86, pp. 203-220, 2000.
[http://dx.doi.org/10.1016/S0167-6105(00)00011-8]

[13] R.P. Hoxey, and P.J. Richard, "Flow pattern and pressure field around a full-scale building", *J. Wind Eng. Ind. Aerodyn.,* vol. 50, pp. 203-212, 1993.
[http://dx.doi.org/10.1016/0167-6105(93)90075-Y]

[14] "FLUENT 2.1.22 help menu",

[15] R.N. Meroney, B.M. Leitl, S. Rafailidis, and M. Schatzmann, "Wind-tunnel and numerical modelling of flow and dispersion about several building shapes", *Journal of Wind Engineering and Industrial Aerodynamics,* vol. 81, Elsevier, pp. 333-345, 1999.

[16] H. Grassmann, F. Bet, M. Ceschia, and M.L. Ganis, "On the physics of partially static turbines", In: *Renewable Energy, 29.* Elsevier, 2003, pp. 491-499.

[17] P.J. Roache, K. Ghia, and F. White, "Editorial policy statement on the control of numerical accuracy", *J. Fluids Eng.,* vol. 108, no. 1, p. 2, 1986.
[http://dx.doi.org/10.1115/1.3242537]

CHAPTER 5

Building-Integrated Wind Turbines

Abstract: Building-integrated wind turbines have special qualities that distinguish them from the entire wind turbines industry, which include the need to be much quieter, while maximising energy generation considering the limited swept area of the turbines. This has inspired a great deal of innovations that need to be investigated and revisited for further improvements across architecturally optimised buildings incorporating wind energy generation or building-integrated wind turbines. The aim is to draw some lessons or perhaps to mimic their principles within suitable architectural forms. One of the lessons learnt from a diffuser design that can be translated into building design to augment wind turbines is the area ratio, *i.e.* ratio of outlet to inlet areas, and length–diameter ratio, *i.e.* ratio of length to diameter. The larger these ratios, the larger the expected power output of the augmented wind turbines will be.

Keywords: Building-integrated wind turbines, Diffusers, Duct augmented wind turbines, Silent wind turbines, Vibration control.

1. INTRODUCTION

There is a specific chapter in this book only on building-integrated wind turbines because majority of the enhancements in architectural designs to meet elevated extents of wind energy generation could be made at the level of individual small wind turbines. As such, they can operate as stand-alone machines or integrated into buildings at some point. Although these individual turbines may be very well engineered to solve several specific issues, it would be sometimes too late for them to be integrated in buildings in the first place, or if they do, they would likely lose out on maximising the potential of the available wind resources for harvesting it, unless the individual turbines are considered as a part of the architectural design from the onset.

These stand-alone turbines or 'building-integrated wind turbines' can be very innovative in solving issues such as noise and vibrations and can maximise the wind velocity to a great extent. Some of these features are discussed in the following sections:

Abdel Rahman Elbakheit
All rights reserved-© 2021 Bentham Science Publishers

2. NOISE REDUCTION OR PREVENTION

'Swift wind turbines' are good examples of addressing the problem of noise in wind turbines. These turbines were originally designed and engineered by the Scottish company, renewable Devices, a resemblance of which is shown in Fig. (**1**). The original 'Swift wind turbine' had five blades made of carbon fibres with an overall diameter of 2.1 m and a distinctive circular outer rim and two positioning blades. This turbine can produce 1.5 kW of electricity from 14 m/s of wind velocity. They work on the principle that the sound generated by the evenly spaced blade tips actually comes from the blade's tips having the maximum rotating speed on the turbine, disturbing the wind molecules at equal intervals (*i.e.* the spacing between the blades). This is how sound waves are generally created in nature [1]. By providing an extra outer rim connecting the tips of the blades, they eliminate the interval gabs that create the rhythmic excitation of the wind molecules. Therefore, reducing or eliminating the noise created by the tips of the blades, which is typically the loudest noise generated by such small-scale turbines. Other inner parts of the blade can also create this noise, but they rotate at a lower velocity and therefore create lesser noise.

Fig. (1). Swift wind turbine with rim around tip of blade. Courtesy of the Scottish company, Renewable Devices.

This noise generated by wind turbines is classified as airborne noise, where the sound is generated and propagated through air. The most efficient way of blocking it, is by total isolation of the air around the source of the noise from the air where occupants reside. Architecturally, this means providing an air-tight building envelope that separate and isolate these two areas of noise generation and noise reception. However, outside the building, the noise would still be present. Therefore, only activities that are not affected by noise could be undertaken outside the buildings.

3. WIND-INDUCED VIBRATIONS IN WIND TURBINES

Wind-induced vibrations in wind turbines can be expressed in two forms:

First, vibrations induced by the mechanical energy resulting from the rotation of the turbines. These vibrations reduce the mechanical energy conversion into electricity and may influence potential faults. Second, vibration induced by the aerodynamic excitation of the structures supporting the turbines. These vibrations result from the uniformity of the support sections and affect the stability of turbines and structures alike.

Moreover, reducing these vibrations can considerably diminish if not eliminate damage to critical parts of wind turbines such as supporting posts, drivetrain, blades and gear [2], if simulated beforehand using computational fluid dynamics, CFD for instance. While vibrations are mostly caused due to aerodynamic behaviour, different parts of the turbines react to the vibrations differently. In addition, different components have different types of vibrations. For example, low-frequency vibrations in the range 0–200Hz are common in the tower post or the main structure, while high-frequency vibrations in the range 3–20 kHz are common in the gear and drivetrain. We can identify the causes of vibrations in different parts according to the steps followed in a previous study [2]:

Tower Post: It is the supporting structure that is usually towering high to support and enable turbines to harvest energy from high-velocity winds. This post may be subjected to vortex shedding that causes vibrations and oscillations due to the uniformity of its cross section. It worth mentioning that tall buildings can function as supports to wind turbines, thereby eliminating the need for separate supports for the turbines.

Turbine Blade: Turbine blades with different pitch angles can produce vibrations in the turbine, accompanying gear and supporting structure, or in any of these components alone. Different pitch angles would also cause an unsteady angular rotational speed.

Vibrations may be severe normally at wind velocities above 12 m/s. This is mainly because of the increase in drag forces at such high wind velocities [3].

The source of vibration could be difficult to detect if not impossible, even with close monitoring, due to the tight connectivity of the turbine parts; therefore, simulations involving mathematical modelling is one of the most promising tools to investigate this issue [3].

4. INCREASING WIND VELOCITY FOR WIND TURBINES

Standalone wind turbines can harvest only a fraction of the power in the wind; this is known as the Betz [4] law or limit, 59.3%. However, researchers have theoretically proved that with the introduction of a nozzle/diffuser casement around a standalone turbine, its power output could be magnified to 3.5 times [5] of conventional standalone wind turbine output. The nozzle is effectively a Venturi tube (discussed in Chapter 2), with its inner and outer sections being transformed in the form of an aerofoil profile. Other terms for this nozzle are diffusers, shrouds or aerofoils.

Perhaps these augmented wind turbines profiles gained their acceptance as viable solutions for boosting conventional wind energy generation during the 'innovative wind systems conference' in the US, 1979 [6].

4.1. Diffuser Design Evolution

The earliest trace to the diffuser technology can be attributed to Lilly and Rainbird, 1956 [7]; in their study, they compared the performance of a 'ducted windmill' with and without duct or shroud based on the one dimensional (1D) momentum theory. They concluded that a 65% increase in the maximum power is possible with a duct of a 3.5 area ratio (*i.e.* outlet to inlet area ratio), with a 15% pressure loss compared to that of conventional mills.

Igra Ozer, 1970 [8], investigated techniques of reducing the requirement of a large length–diameter ratio in a diffuser without affecting the performance. Igra provided air inlets on the latter-side of the diffuser (Fig. **2**). He also used a straight-walled diffuser with a series of drilled-in ports, an aerofoil and a flat plate ring at the exit. One of the conclusions drawn is that bleeding air (in or out) did not improve flow separation, while blowing air in within the high-pressure region increased power output by 20%. Moreover, using an aerofoil ring flap increased power by 65% (Fig. **2**).

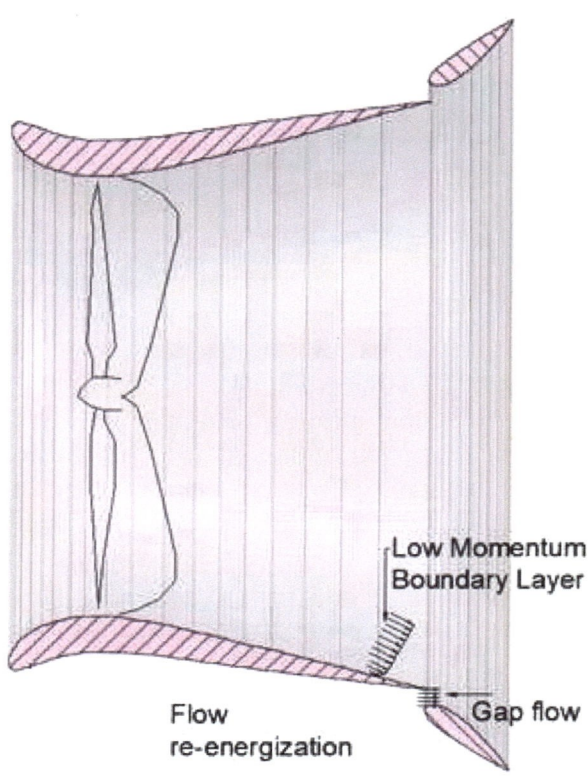

Fig. (2). Igra's diffuser with flow re-energisation flaps [8].

The importance of the aerofoil design in providing an extra lift force compared to flat diffusers, which lack this additional lift, is significant. This lift force increases the mass flow rate inside the diffuser of a given length–diameter ratio. However, flat diffusers have the advantage of less material weight, low costs and reliability.

Other factors that contribute in diffuser design and performance are the area ratio, length–diameter ratio, pressure drop in the turbine, pressure recovery at the diffuser exit, tip speed ratio (*i.e.*, ratio of tip speed to main streem speed), disk loading and pressure coefficient.

4.2. Technical Background

The 1D actuator disk theory, also called the 1D momentum theory, presents the energy balance in the diffuser using Bernoulli's equations and depicts the momentum balance [9]. This theory does not consider the wake turbulence, the number of blades or aerodynamic drag. The diffuser can be split into four regions (Fig. 3) [10]:

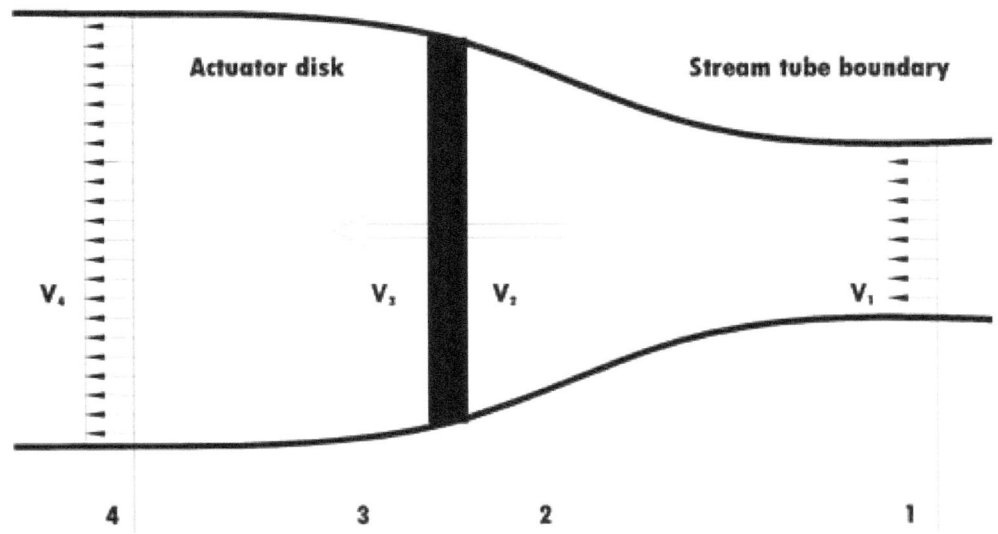

Fig. (3). Control volume of the actuator disk model of the wind turbine.

1. Inlet (upstream before the diffuser).
2. The region in front of the turbine.
3. The region just behind the turbine.
4. Outlet (exit, which is a faraway region).

In steady state and since momentum is conserved, thrust is equal to the change in momentum, and mass flow is conserved.

$$F_{thrust} = V_1(\rho A V)_1 - V_4(\rho A V)_4, \quad (1)$$

where ρ is the air density, A is the rotor disk cross-sectional area and V is the air flow velocity.

For a steady flow,

$$\dot{m} = (\rho A V)_1 = (\rho A V)_4 \quad F_{thrust} = \dot{m}(V_1 - V_4) \quad (2)$$

It is assumed that the pressure far upstream, P1, and that far downstream, P4, are equal, P1 = P4. The velocity on both sides of the turbine is considered to be equal, V2 = V3.

$$F_{thrust} = A2(P2 - P3) \qquad (3)$$

The velocity at the turbine, V2, is found to be the mean of V1 and V4.

$$V2 = \tfrac{1}{2}(V1 - V4) \text{ (4)} \qquad (4)$$

The axial induction factor, a, indicates the drop in velocity from the upstream to the turbine position.

$$a = \left(\frac{(V1 - V2)}{V1}\right) \qquad (5)$$

The maximum value for $a = \tfrac{1}{2}$ and requires the velocity V3 behind the turbine to be zero. Then, the thrust would be represented as follows:

$$F_{thrust} = \tfrac{1}{2}\rho A V_1^2 \,[4a(1-a)] \qquad (6)$$

The power coefficient is the ratio of the power extracted to the total power available and can be defined in terms of *a* as follows:

$$C_p = 4a(1-a)^2 \qquad (7)$$

The maximum value for power coefficient C_p is 0.593, which called the Betz limit as discussed earlier in section 5, and it occurs at a= 1/3.

4.3. Velocity and Pressure of the Diffuser

As shown in the previous sections, the velocity and pressure in the diffuser are a direct result of the shape of the diffuser. The area ratio of the diffuser β is equal to V_2/V_4, and the exit area of the diffuser must be larger in area than the inlet area to maximise performance and reduce turbulence. The backpressure velocity ratio is defined as ϒ, which is equal to V_4/V_1. This implies that the exit velocity V_4 differs from the inlet velocity V_1.

The inlet should be designed in a way to reduce resistance and to allow for a smooth transition of the flow and avoid separation. The flow will find resistance from the turbine, which is why it should be placed at the shorted cross section of the diffuser to reduce resistance to the flow [11]. The amount of air flow rate increase through the turbine in a diffuser is β·ϒ times greater than that passing through the bare turbine of the same swept area.

4.4. Classifications of Ducted Wind Turbines

Ducted wind turbines are normal wind turbines but with a duct, diffuser or shroud, around them (Fig. **4**). They can be classified according to the type or shape of the duct. However, all ducts accelerate the air velocity, increasing energy production from turbines, reducing wind intermittences and streamlining the air flow. Therefore, the capacity factor of the turbines can be increased. Some shrouds or diffusers are equipped with rotational capability for capturing frequent wind direction changes. Diffusers are available normally for small- to medium-sized turbines. They are generally suitable for locations such as roadsides, rooftops, fields and gardens. Although larger diffusers are also available, they require additional mechanical and structural supports, such as gear boxes or supporting pylons.

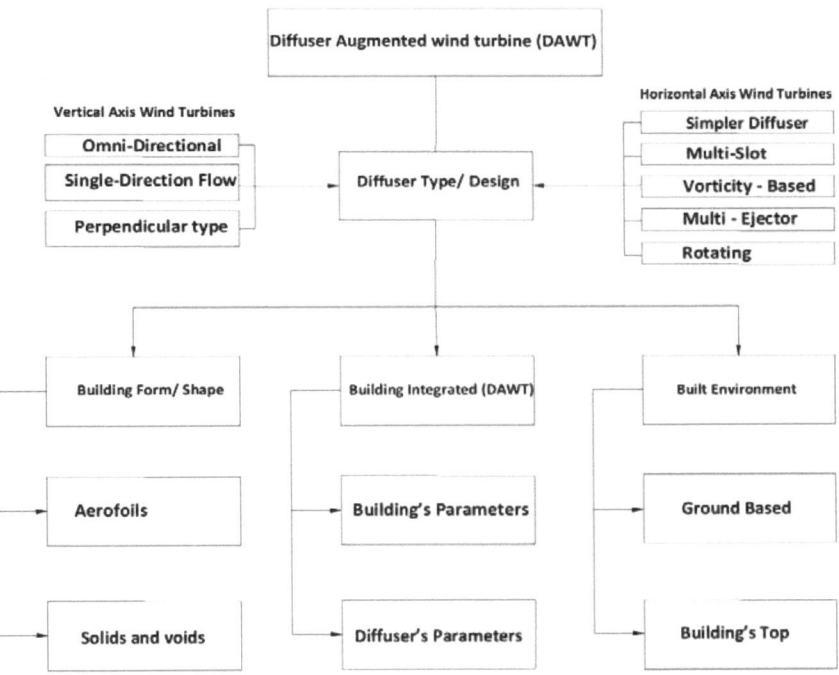

Fig. (4). Types of diffusers for augmented wind turbines.

Fig. (**4**) above depicts the main types of diffusers that can be incorporated in turbines used for buildings. They can be incorporated in both vertical-axis and horizontal-axis wind turbines. However, vertical-axis wind turbines have a limited variety of diffusers compared to the horizontal-axis wind turbines. Only omnidirectional, single direction or perpendicular diffusers available for vertical-axis wind turbines, whereas simple, multi-slot, vorticity-based and rotating diffusers along with multi-ejectors are available for horizontal-axis wind turbines. When it comes to building integration, Diffusers can either be used for infrastructures such as roads, streets, bridges or simply on the ground, or they can be integrated into buildings at some point in the future. Alternatively, they can also be integrated into the design of the buildings from the start, which would allow better control of wind resources, enabling more favourable results to be anticipated.

Descriptions of some of diffuser types are given in Fig. (**4**):

4.4.1. Simple Diffusers

Simple diffusers vary in their cross-sectional profile, from aerodynamically influenced to simple straight sections (Fig. **5**). In addition, they vary in area ratio, cross-section to length ratio and diameter. However, they all have a converging entry and a diverging exit, as well as a blade clearance of at least 2%.

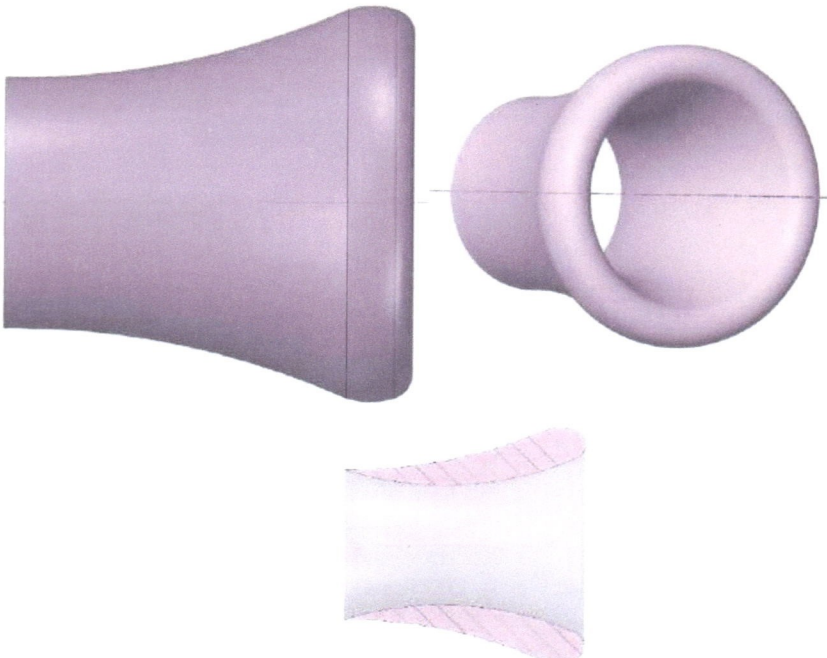

Fig. (5). Simple diffuser with an aerodynamic section.

4.4.2. Multi-slot Diffuser

The aim of this diffuser is to introduce more outside air into the wake area of the diffuser, thus increasing the air velocity at the exit based on the Bernoulli effect. This would produce even lower pressures in the wake area of the diffuser (*i.e.* Venturi effect), therefore drawing more air mass flow into the front side where the turbines are located [12].

Fig. (**6**) shows this design. Another advantage of the multi-slot diffuser is that it reduces the needed large diameter–length ratio. Wood patented the multi-slot diffuser design with one or more diffuser rings that channel air to the back of diffuser as noted above [13].

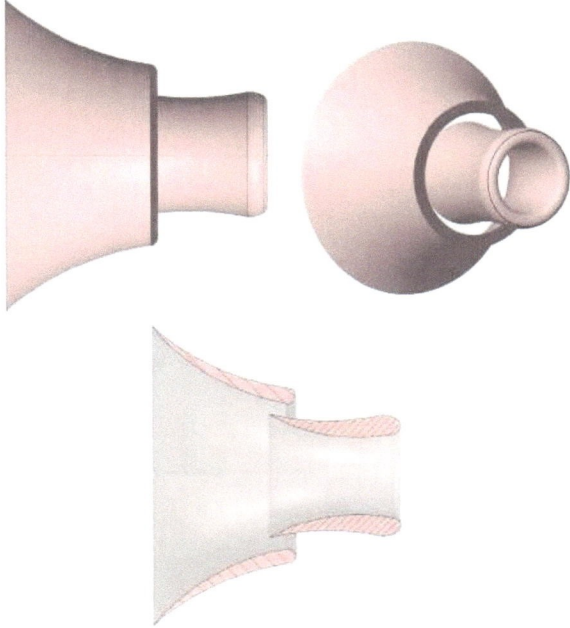

Fig. (6). Multi-slot diffuser.

4.4.3. Brim or Flange Diffuser

This diffuser (Fig. **7**) was discovered by Ohya and Karasudani [14], who called it 'Wind-lens', when they researched about vortex formation and shedding. They realised that unlike the main trend of research on vortex shedding, which was to reduce its formation in order to preserve structural stability and to reduce structural loads. Vortexes that formed out of a brim or flange behind the shrouding wind turbines can actually increase mass flow into the turbines, thus augmenting its energy generation. Tests were conducted to determine the most compact design with highest power augmentation. The design in Fig. (**7**) achieved 2.6 times the power augmentation over a bare turbine. Moreover, vortexes formed by the brim flange lasted for less time compared to those formed by their counter parts from other structures. They concluded that with increasing length–diameter ratio, more power augmentation will result. However, with medium to slightly large turbines and low diffuser lengths, a reduction in power augmentation could result. However, this reduction can be compensated with an increase in the flange height.

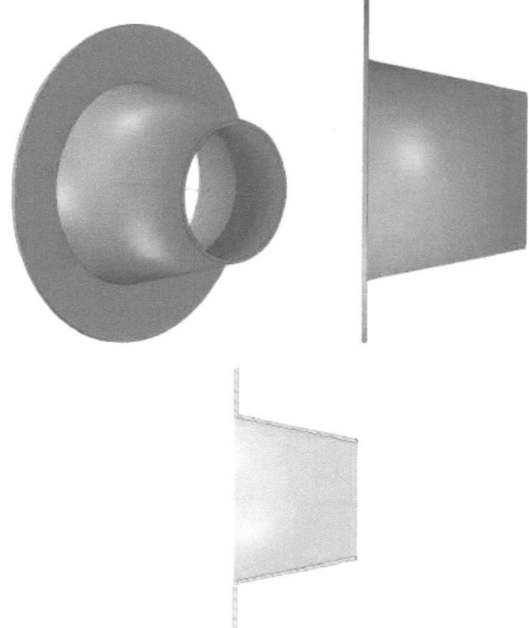

Fig. (7). Brim/flanged diffuser.

4.4.4. Vorticity-based Diffuser/Turbine

This type of diffuser (Fig. **8**) operates with the same principles as those of the brim/flange diffuser in employing vortex formation behind the flange to create a low-pressure area that draws more mass flow rate into the turbine. However, instead of using a flange, it uses a wider angle of the exit of the diffuser and therefore a higher area ratio (*i.e.* outlet area/inlet area). Presumably, this wider angle of the diffuser exit creates circumferential velocity acceleration that draw more wind through the inlet of the diffuser. However, this diffuser needs special blades for turbines to capture the wind flow.

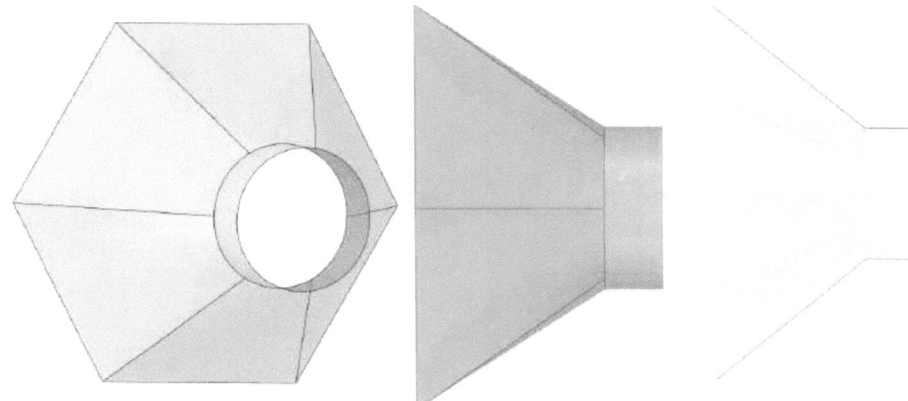

Fig. (8). Vorticity-based diffusers.

Okhio *et al* experimented with a wide diffuser outlet creating circumferential speed to overcome flow separation in the wake area of the diffuser with an open angle of 16.5° and area ratio of 4.4 [15]. They succeeded in maintaining a visual appearance to flow performance. One of their findings is that increasing swirl above a certain point eliminated flow separation, but it also gave rise to central dissipation that increased losses.

Mariotti *et al* examined three Diffusers with an area ratio of 2, but different divergence half-angles of 2°, 3.5° and 5°, which were subjected to induced local recirculations along the diffuser walls [16]. At half-angle of 2°, the flow remained attached to the diverging walls. However, for the other two larger half-angles, asymmetrical recirculation occurred at diverging wall. The addition of an optimised cavity helped in reducing pressure losses to the flow and increasing reattachment of the flow.

4.4.5. Mixer Ejector Wind Turbine

This is a technology that is a blend of a diffuser and ejector, which is used to propel wind turbines further (Fig. **9**) through single and multi-stage ejector technology beyond the Betz limit. Presz *et al* patented a mixer ejector turbine that has an air intake similar to that of an aircraft jet enforced by a multi-slot air intake behind the turbine as a second stage [17]. The multi-slot air intake introduces more natural pressured air to the low-pressure area behind the turbine, thus accelerating air more through the turbine. Power augmentation is predicted to be 3–4 times that of a bare turbine.

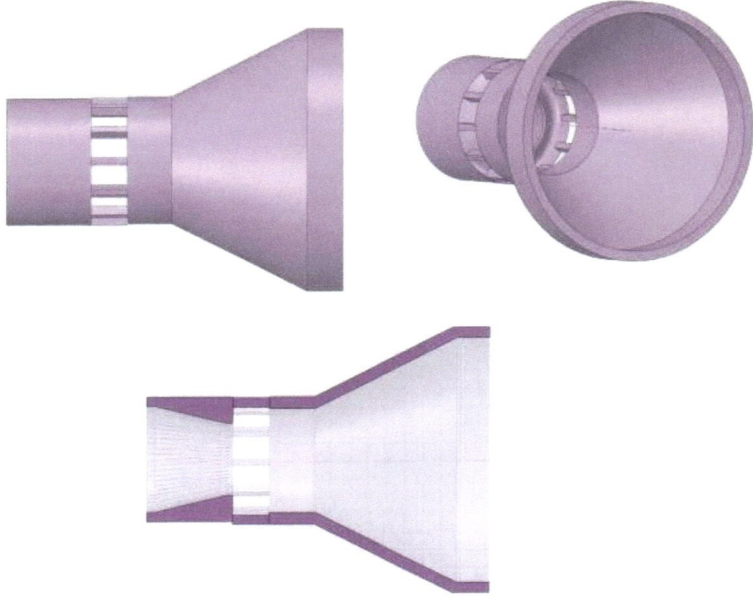

Fig. (9). Mixer ejector diffuser.

4.4.6. Rotating Diffuser

In this type, the diffuser is fixed to the end of turbine rotor and rotates with it (Fig. (**10**); therefore, it is also referred to as a dynamic diffuser. Anakata - Wind Power Resources patented a rotating diffuser [18]. The fact that the diffuser is attached to the turbine tip blades reduces vibrations of the turbine. These turbines are usually made of acrylic, which is an easy-to-replace and a light-weight material. However, it is not clear whether this would increase turbine drag.

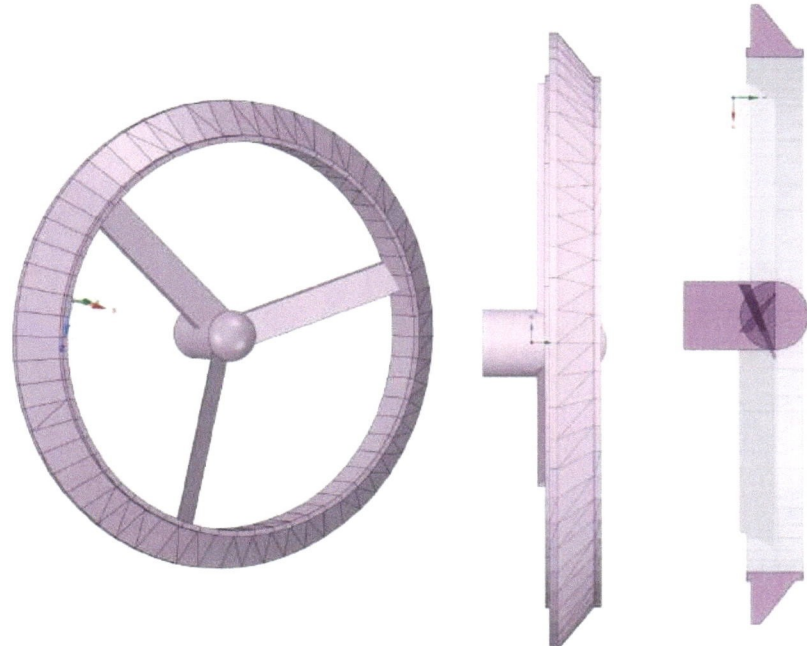

Fig. (10). Rotating diffusers.

CONCLUSION

Power augmentation of energy generation from wind turbines can be achieved through the use of diffusers of different designs with 2–3 times more energy output than that of standalone turbines. However, simple designs can be easily implemented to various types of turbine designs and sizes. One of the lessons learnt from the diffuser designs that could be translated into building designs to augment wind turbines is the importance of the area ratio and length–diameter ratio. The larger these ratios, the larger the expected power augmentations of wind turbines will be.

REFERENCES

[1] B.J. Smith, R.J. Peters, and S. Owen, "Acoustics and noise control", In: *Longman*, 1996.

[2] A.R. Elbakheit, "Wind-induced vibrations to tall buildings and wind turbines", [http://dx.doi.org/10.5772/intechopen.72094]

[3] P.G.D. Infield, "Wind turbine tower vibration modelling and monitoring by the nonlinear state estimation technique (NSET)", *Energies,* pp. 5279-5293, 2012.

[4] A. Betz, *Introduction to the theory of flow machines.* Pergamon Press: Oxford, New York, 1966.

[5] B. Franković, and I. Vrsalović, "New high profitable wind turbines", *Renew. Energy,* vol. 24, no. 3, pp. 491-499, 2001.

[http://dx.doi.org/10.1016/S0960-1481(01)00033-7]

[6] A.A. Agha, H.N. Chaudhry, and F. Wang, "Diffuser augmented wind turbine (DAWT) technologies: a review", *International J Renewable Energy Research,* vol. 8, no. 3, pp. 1369-1385, 2018.

[7] G.M. Lilley, and W.J. Rainbird, *A preliminary report on the design and performance of ducted windmills.* College of Aeronautics: Cranfield, 1956.

[8] V.V. Dighe, F. Avallone, O. Igra, and G. van Bussel, "Multi-element ducts for ducted wind turbines: a numerical study", *Wind Energy Science,* vol. 4, pp. 439-449, 2019.
[http://dx.doi.org/10.5194/wes-4-439-2019]

[9] L. Dhakshinamurhty, Rameshkumar, B. Navaneeth, and R. Kirubakaran, "Design and analysis of diffuser augmented wind turbine using CFD", *Wind Energy Science,* no. 4, p. 439p. 449, 2019.

[10] D. Zhao, N. Han, E. Goh, J. Cater, and A. Reinecke, "Chapter 1 - general introduction to wind turbines", In: *Wind Turbines and Aerodynamics Energy Harvesters* vol. 6. Academic Press, 2019, pp. 1-20.

[11] S.Z. Roshan, S. Alimirzazadeh, and M. Rad, "RANS simulations of the stepped duct effect on the performance of ducted wind turbine", *J. Wind Eng. Ind. Aerodyn.,* vol. 145, pp. 270-279, 2015.
[http://dx.doi.org/10.1016/j.jweia.2015.07.010]

[12] K.M. Foreman, B. Gilbert, and R.A. Oman, "Diffuser augmentation of wind turbines", *Sol. Energy,* vol. 20, no. 4, pp. 305-311, 1978.
[http://dx.doi.org/10.1016/0038-092X(78)90122-6]

[13] B.D.O. Wood, "Diffuser augmented wind turbines", *Anakata Wind Power Resources s.a.r.l. (Corcelles, CH). Patent Application No.9512817,* United States, 2016.

[14] Y.a.K. Ohya, "Shrouded wind turbine generating high output power with wind-lens technology", *Energies,* vol. 3, pp. 634-649, 2010.
[http://dx.doi.org/10.3390/en3040634]

[15] C.B. Okhio, H.P. Horton, and G. Langer, "Effects of swirl on flow separation and performance of wide angle diffusers", *Int. J. Heat Fluid Flow,* vol. 4, no. 4, pp. 199-206, 1983.
[http://dx.doi.org/10.1016/0142-727X(83)90039-5]

[16] A. Mariotti, G. Buresti, and M. Salvetti, "Use of multiple local recirculations to increase the efficiency in diffusers", *Eur. J. Mech. BFluids,* p. 50, 2014.

[17] W.M.W. Presz, "Wind turbine with mixers and ejectors", In: *Flodesign Wind Turbine Corporation (Wilbraham, MA, US). Patent Application No.8021100, United States,* 2011.

[18] W.E. Rushing, "Anakata - wind power resources", *UK,* 2014.

CHAPTER 6

Effect of Turbine Resistance and Positioning on the Performance of Aerofoil Building-Augmented Wind Energy Generation

Abstract: In this chapter, more insight into the benefits of aerofoils and their integration into architectural forms to further enhance wind energy generation is investigated. More light is shed on wind flows around and under the aerofoil, when introducing turbines as resistance to flow under aerofoils. Turbine resistance is introduced using porous jump in CFD ANSYS FLUENT. The estimated energy generation is calculated based on the resulting wind velocities, pressure drop and area per square metre. In general, resistance from turbines lowered the resulting wind velocities; however, this reduction was the lowest for the optimised case (Chapter 4). The resulting wind velocity was 13.2 m/s for optimised case and 10.85 m/s for the unoptimised case. In addition, the optimised case exhibited a greater pressure drop across the turbine than that of the unoptimised case, thus producing 1.6–1.9 times more energy than that of the unoptimised case. For the same cases, an increase in energy production of up to 3.38 times is obtained by appropriately placing the turbine (*i.e.* 2 m from the tip of the aerofoil on the windward side) [1].

Keywords: Aerofoils, Architectural forms, BAWES, Building-augmented wind energy systems, Building-integrated wind turbines, CFD, Duct-augmented wind turbines, Wind energy optimisation.

1. INTRODUCTION

Renewable energy technologies are increasingly developing to become the next primary sources of energy worldwide [2]. This is especially evident with the promise it holds for solving some of the most pressing problems facing the globe (IPCC 2014 annual report [2]), such as increased CO_2 emissions, increased energy demands and continuous population growth. Renewable energy sources such as wind, solar, geothermal and tidal energies can significantly contribute to this.

Owning to the high energy demand from the built environment, which amounts to higher than 60% of the global energy demand, great efforts are in dire need to provide reliable sustainable options to satisfy such a large share of energy demand. Moreover, the high potential of wind energy generation complements the requirements of the built environment in terms of versatile perspectives, such as availability, accessibility, reliability and return on investments. This appears to be a very plausible option to purse. In this regard, small-scale wind turbines provide a very promising option for the built environments. However, several obstacles must be combated, such as very low wind velocities to be harvested and the variability of wind patterns or turbulence. Few remedies to these problems already exist, which are architectural forms, aerofoils and shrouds [3].

The choice of architectural forms, building massing, solids and voids in buildings' forms have great influence on wind patterns at a certain location. Aerofoils and shrouds are fixed shapes designed to channel wind around buildings and reduce turbulence, while accelerating wind flow [4]. Turbines are normally fixed in between aerofoils and buildings. Aerofoils provide further enhancement to the environment around buildings by reducing noise levels from turbines, protecting the buildings in the event of blade detachment and enhancing the appearance of buildings. Further investigation into the wind velocity augmentation by means of aerofoils is undertaken in this chapter. Following on the discussion in Chapter 4 and using the same building design of a detached house described in that chapter, this investigation was conducted.

2. EFFECT OF TURBINE RESISTANCE ON RESULTING VELOCITIES AND FLOW PATTERNS

To examine turbine resistance to the flow under an aerofoil, a turbine is simulated as a pressure drop surface by means of a porous jump boundary condition in ANSYS FLUENT. Initially the turbine is positioned at the shortest distance between the aerofoil and roof at 3.39 m to the right of the aerofoil.

'Turbine resistance' or 'blockage effect' are two terms denoting the same effect, which is how a turbine is obstructing wind flow. This obstruction applies more for drag type turbines than for lift type turbines.

This parameter is calculated as $\frac{A^T}{A^T - A^F}$, where A^T is the space below the aerofoil and A^F is the turbine swept area.

Two main scenarios are followed. The first is the optimised case with the aerofoil placed 85 cm from the roof surface with an angle of attack of 50°. The second is the base case of investigation, wherein the aerofoil is placed 220 cm from the roof surface with an angle of attack of 20°. The study compared these cases with and without turbine resistance effect. As a result, two categories of results were obtained:

2.1. Effect of Turbine Resistance on Wind Flow Patterns

We know that the shape of the aerofoil is the main determinant of the flow around it, specifically the angle of attack and the aerofoil's distance from the roof [3]. In Figs. (**1** and **2**), the flow patterns around the aerofoil are compared for two scenarios. The optimised case is shown in Fig. (**1**), and the unoptimised in Fig. (**2**). Furthermore, for each case, an additional case with turbine resistance is incorporated with the ensuing wind pattern revealed.

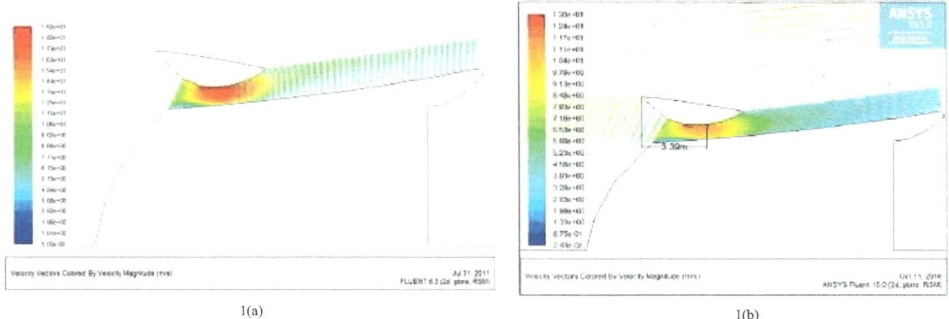

1(a)   1(b)

Fig. (1). Optimised aerofoil **(a)** with no turbine resistance and **(b)** with turbine resistance: 90% blockage effect.

In these figures, the following have been noted:

First, less pronounced separation and therefore lower resistance to flow was observed in the optimised case compared to those in the unoptimised case.

Second, better acceleration is noted in the optimised case than that in the unoptimised case, despite the fact that both have improvement in wind velocity or acceleration as Tables **1** and **2** reveal.

Table 1. Effect of turbine resistance below the aerofoil (turbine simulated with porous jump).

Case	Mean Velocity. m/s	Max. Velocity m/s	Pressure Coefficient Cp
Optimised	10.44	13.2	−82.03
Unoptimised	9.90	10.85	−40.41

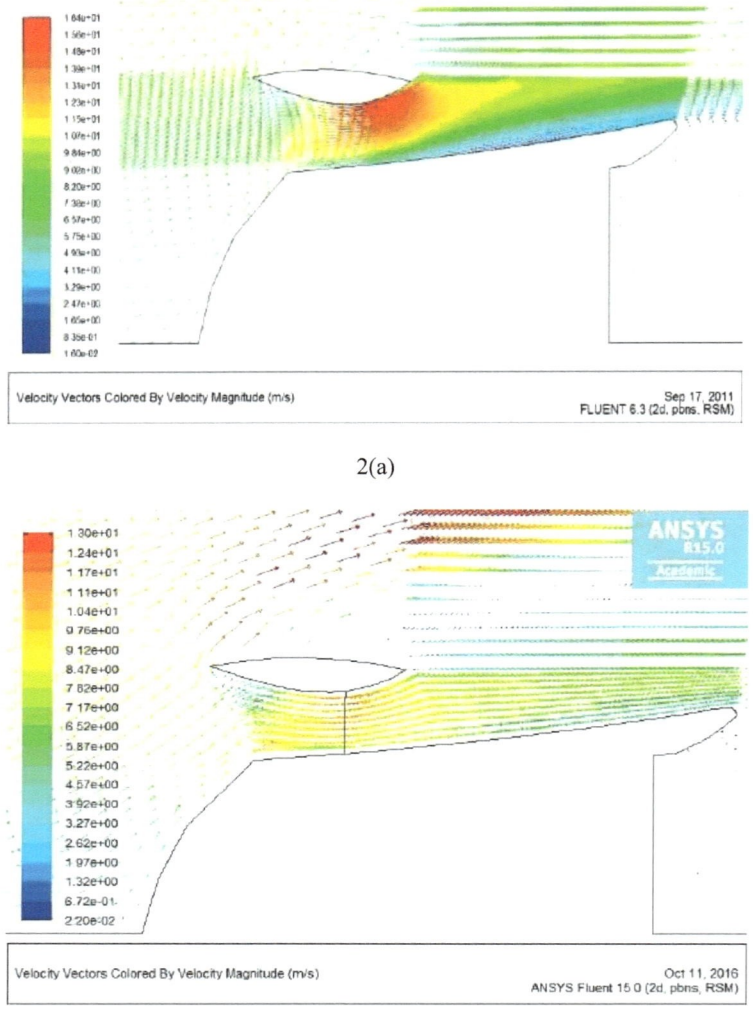

2(a)

2(b)

Fig. (2). Unoptimised aerofoil **(a)** with no turbine resistance and **(b)** with turbine resistance: 90% blockage effect.

Table 2. Effect of turbine resistance under the aerofoil (no turbine is included).

Case	Mean Velocity m/s	Max. Velocity m/s	Pressure Coefficient Cp
Optimised	13.76	19.2	−281.94
Unoptimised	12.8	16.53	−168.0

Third, wind accelerates under the aerofoil in the entire space between it and the roof, far better in the optimised case than in the unoptimised case, wherein a one-sided acceleration just below the aerofoil is observed (Fig. 1). Such flows may be best suited for vertical-axis wind turbines and Savonious wind turbines for instance.

Fourth, wind flow patterns under the aerofoil changed considerably by eliminating recirculation on top of the roof in the leeward side of the space behind the aerofoil, as observed for both cases without turbine resistance (Fig. **1(a)** and Fig. **(2(a))**. This recirculation is removed entirely by the addition of the turbine resistance (Figs. **1b** and **2b**). This is in agreement with the findings from previous studies [4].

2.2. Effect of Turbine Resistance on Resulting Wind Velocities

First, turbine resistance under the aerofoil lowered the resulting simulated wind velocity. However, this reduction was lower in the optimised cases compared to that in the unoptimised cases. The optimised case achieved wind velocity of 13.2 m/s, whereas the unoptimised case achieved 10.85 m/s, as shown in Table **1**. Figs. (**3a** and **3b**) show a linear curve depicting the relation between the incident and resulting wind velocities under the aerofoil for both optimised and unoptimised cases. However, the optimised cases have higher resulting wind velocities as a consequence of controlled separation.

Furthermore, Fig. (**3a**) reveals that for the optimised case under higher percentages of porosity (*i.e.* with lower turbine resistance), higher resulting velocities are achieved, whereas for the unoptimised cases, all porosity percentages achieved the same resulting velocities without considerable variation.

Second, turbine resistance reduced pressure drop across the turbine (*i.e.* porous jump plane) as it produced −82.03 Pa for the optimised case, while it was −281.94 Pa for the same case without turbine resistance or porous jump. The unoptimised case produced −40.41 Pa with the porous jump. Fig. (**4**) portrays the entire picture of pressure distribution around the optimised aerofoil with the turbine resistance (*i.e.* porous jump plane) integrated. It can be observed that the pressure is pretty high on the windward side of the aerofoil (*i.e.* the left side of Fig. (**4**) and drops considerably after the porous jump plane (*i.e.* the right side of Fig. (**4**). The pressure is further reduced to about −13.2 Pa in the further leeward side of the turbine.

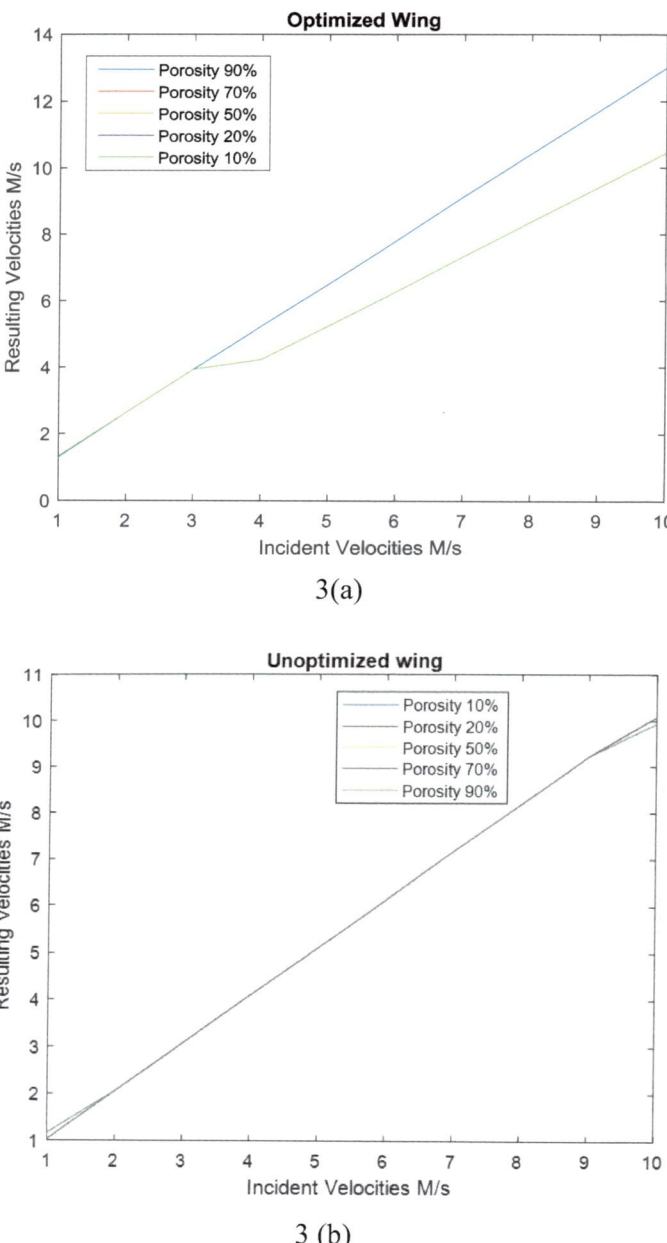

Fig. (3). Resulting velocities under different porosity percentages in **(a)** optimised aerofoil and **(b)** unoptimised aerofoil.

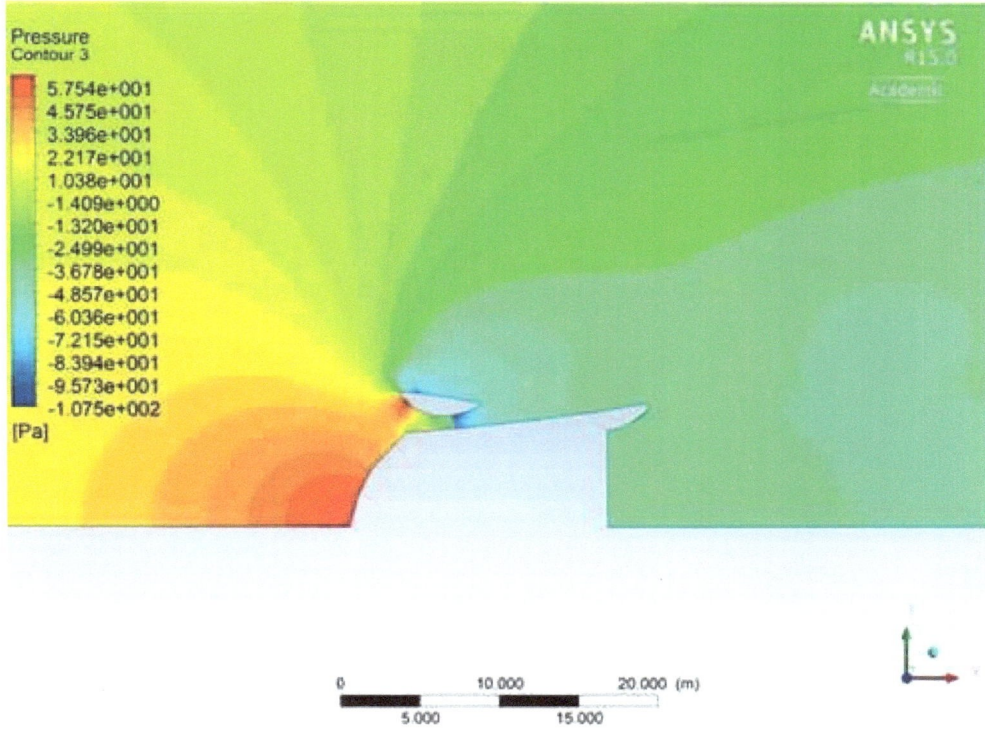

Fig. (4). Contours of pressure coefficient distribution around optimised aerofoil and porous jump plane.

Third, the mean resulting wind velocity and pressure drop across the turbine (*i.e.* porous jump plane) was constant, regardless of changes in the porosity percentages for a single incident wind velocity, as shown in Table **3**.

Table 3. Effect of varying turbine resistance on the mean resulting wind velocity and pressure drop under the aerofoil for an incident wind velocity of 10 m/s.

Turbine Resistance (Percentage of Porosity) %	10%	20%	50%	70%	90%
Mean resulting wind velocities (m/s)	10.44	10.44	10.44	10.44	10.44
Resulting pressure drop (Pa)	−43.98	−43.98	−43.98	−43.98	−43.98

3. EFFECT OF TURBINE RESISTANCE ON RESULTING PRESSURE COEFFICIENT

Additional inspection into the resulting pressure drop due to incorporation of turbines under the aerofoil for the optimised case is presented in Fig. (**5**).

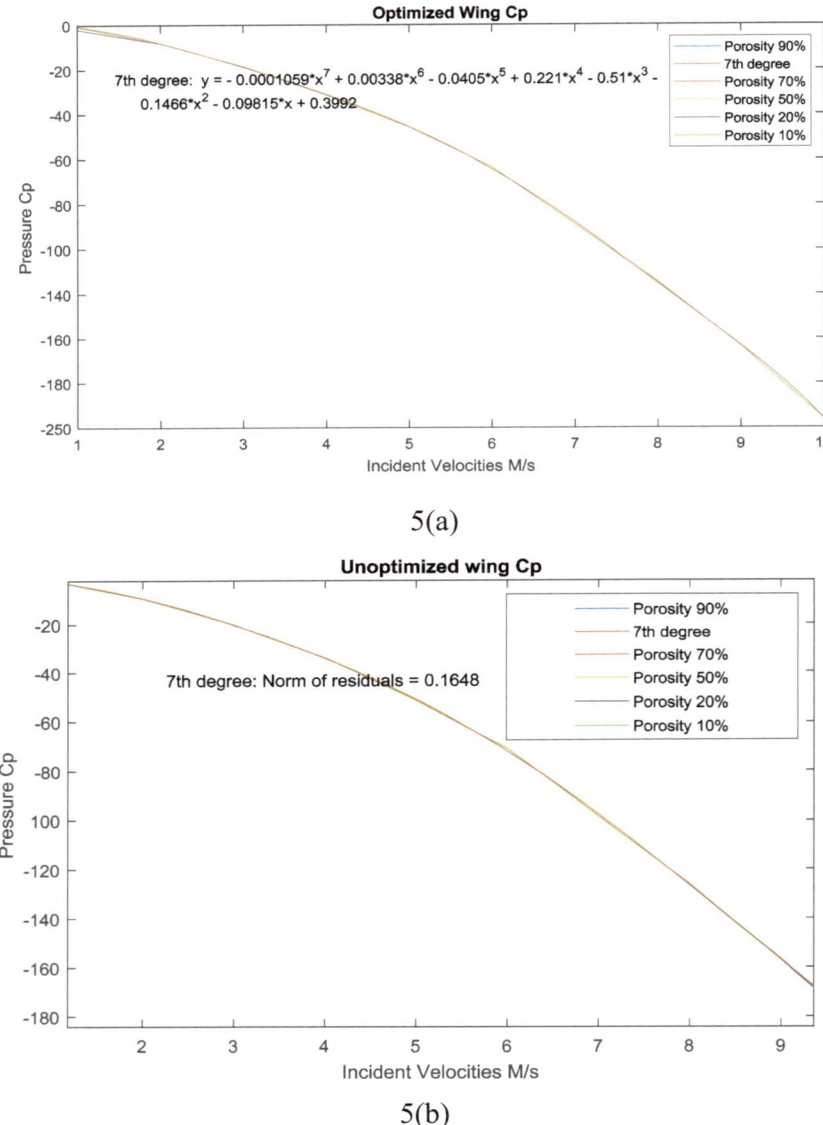

Fig. (5). The resulting pressure coefficient under different porosity percentages for the **(a)** optimised aerofoil and **(b)** unoptimised aerofoil.

In Fig. (5), we can see a comparison between the pressure coefficients of the optimised and unoptimised cases as a result of adding turbine resistance under the aerofoil. It can be concluded that the optimised case exhibited a higher pressure drop across the turbine, and therefore, a higher power yield was estimated. However, both cases provided very subtle variations in pressure drop with the increase of porosity percentages, while significant increase in pressure drop is experienced with increase in incident wind velocities in both cases.

4. EFFECT OF TURBINE RESISTANCE ON RESULTING POWER GENERATION

The estimated power generation after introducing turbines under the aerofoil could be calculated as a result of the pressure drop and the incident wind velocities per square metre of the space of the porous jump. Accordingly, the estimated power from the optimised case is 823 W/m^2, while that from unoptimised case is 400 W/m^2. This is calculated by multiplying 'the area weighted average' resulting wind velocity under the aerofoil, which was 10.44 m/s for the optimised case and 9.9 m/s for the unoptimised case, as presented in Tables **1** and **2**. Additional power would be estimated if we considered using the highest resulting wind velocity from the same tables above Tables (**1** and **2**). This would afford 917.6 W/m^2 for the optimised case and 438.4 W/m^2 for the unoptimised case. The maximum resulting wind velocities were 13.2 m/s, and 10.85 m/s, respectively.

Fig. (**6**) describes the entire picture of the estimated energy generated by turbines under both the optimised and unoptimised cases. A moderate exponential relation between the increase in the incident wind velocity and the estimated power generated was observed as dictated by the wind power equation. However, the optimised case produced far better results into few multiples of thousands Watts/m^2, while the unoptimised into few multiples of hundreds Watts/m^2. Fig. (**7**) shows that as the incident wind velocity increases, there is a rapid decrease in incremental power up to a point where it gets steady, Which is 5 m/s for both cases, where the decrease in incremental power stablises. However, steady power generation is experienced from around 8 m/s, and prior to this there is a slight decrease.

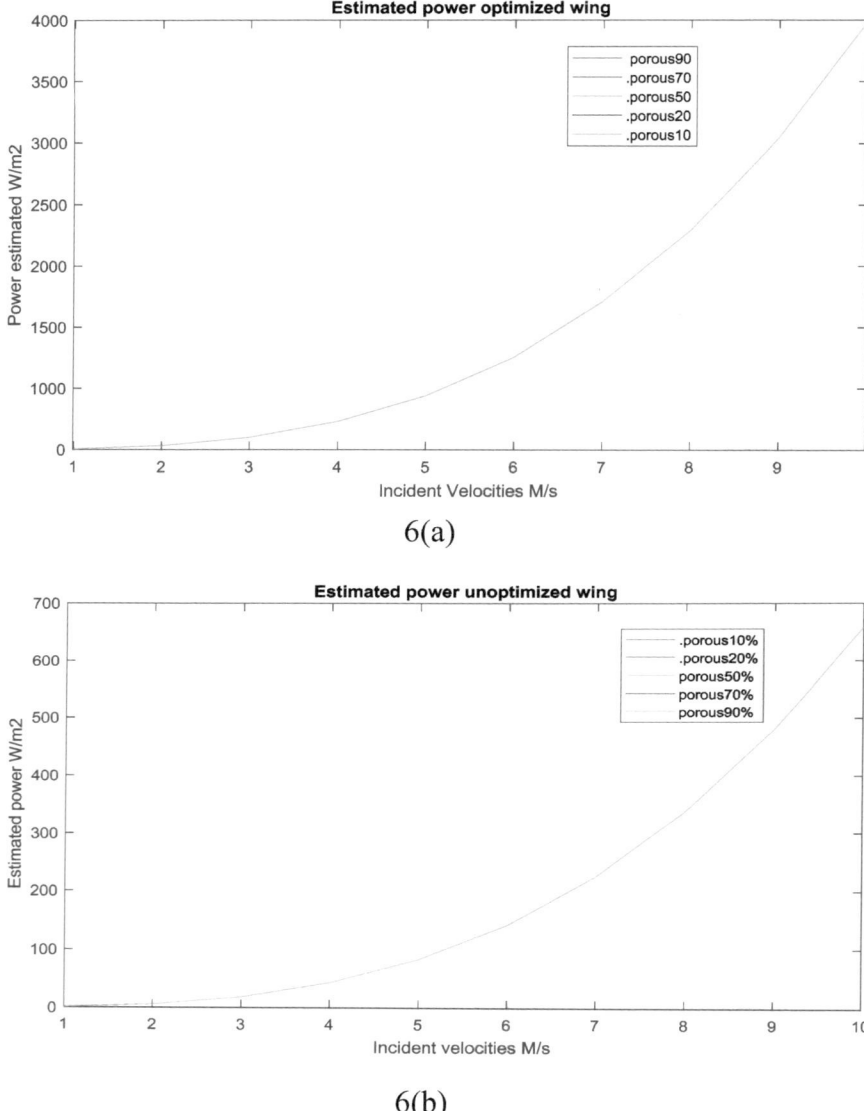

Fig. (6). Estimated power generation under **(a)** optimised aerofoil and **(b)** unoptimised aerofoil.

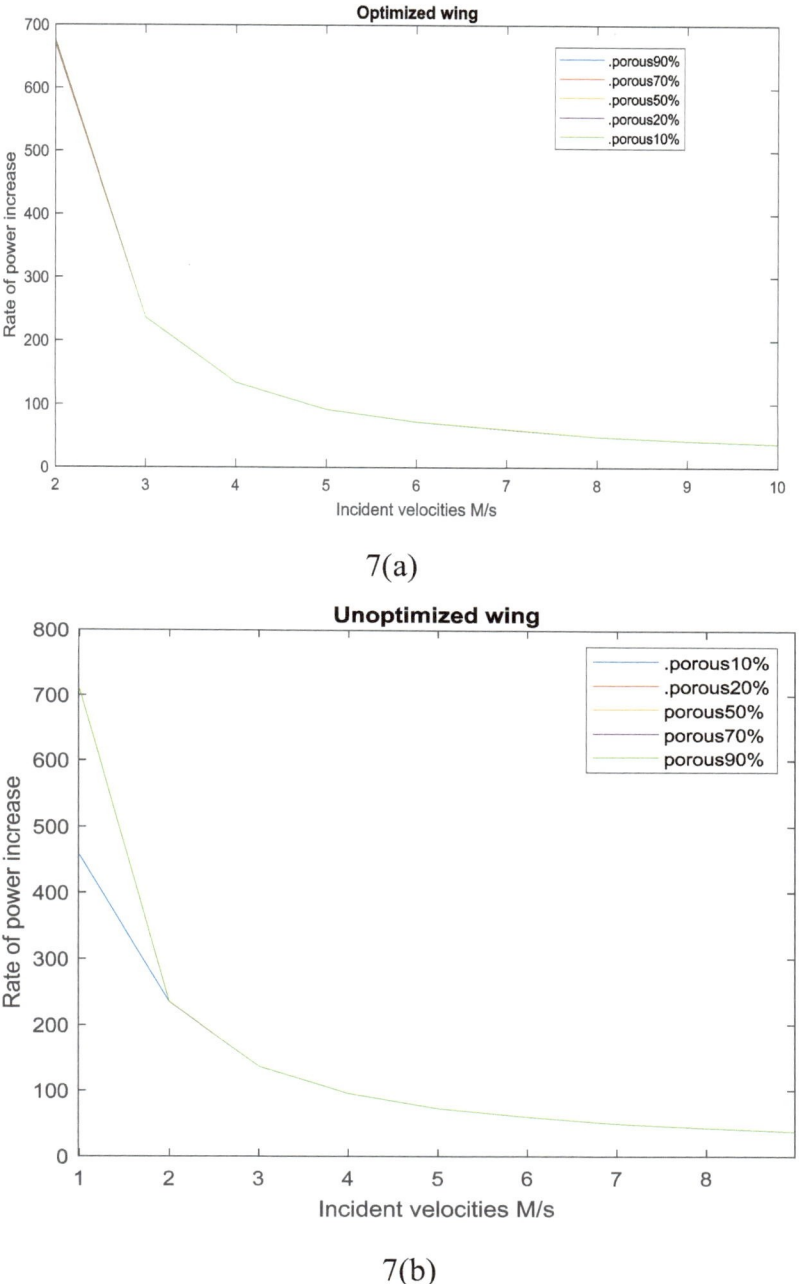

Fig. (7). Rate of power increase under **(a)** optimised aerofoil and **(b)** unoptimised aerofoil.

5. TURBINE POSITIONS UNDER THE AEROFOIL

Two turbines positions are selected to examine the effect of turbine positioning on its power output under the aerofoil. The first position is near the start of the aerofoil (2 m to the right of the left tip of the aerofoil) and the other towards the rear of the aerofoil (3.39 m to the right of the left tip of the aerofoil). The in-between positions are already covered in the previous sections. Fig. (**8**) shows that the former position afforded a higher pressure coefficient than the latter position, which were 153.7 Cp and −61.7 Cp, respectively. However, the resulting wind velocities under the aerofoil for both positions were 8.8 m/ and 11.2 m/s, respectively.

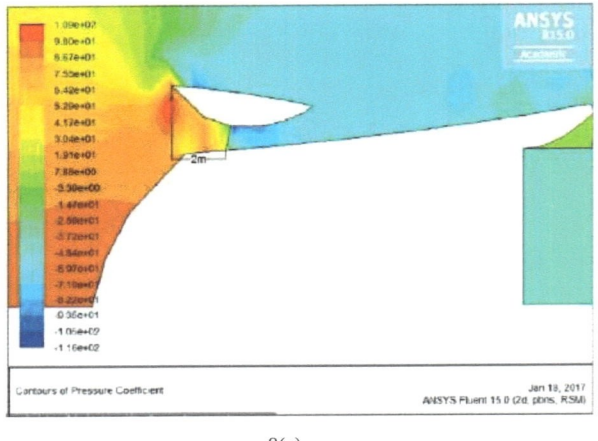

8(a)

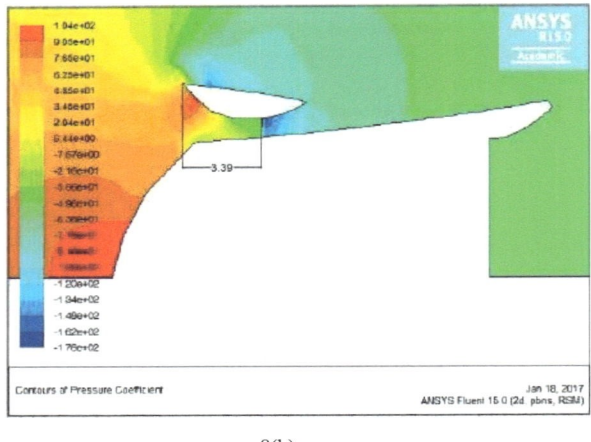

8(b)

Fig. (8). Turbine positioning on the **(a)** windward side and the **(b)** leeward side.

From the values of the pressure coefficient generated and the resulting wind velocities, we can estimate the power resulting at these points as 1352.56 W/m² for the former and 691 W/m² for the latter. Therefore, the former position could generate nearly twice as much energy as that generated by the latter position. When comparing the power generation estimation, we find that the former position produces 3.38 times over than that yielded by the initial unoptimised case.

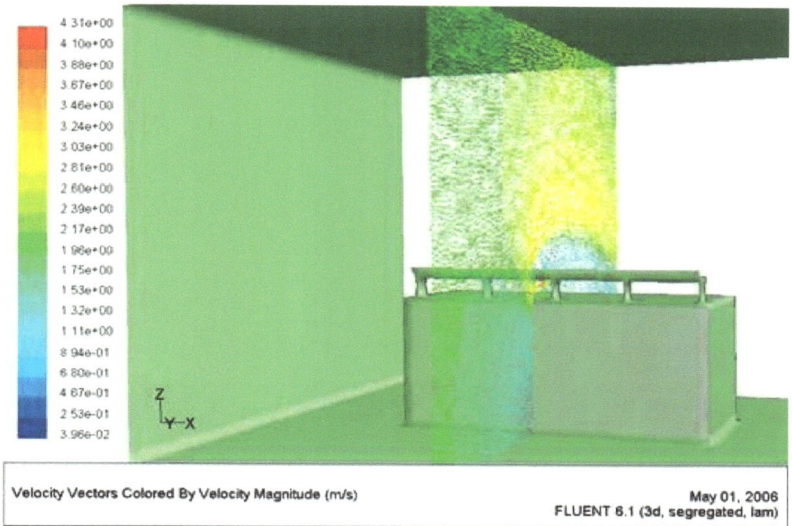

Fig. (9). Velocity vectors for building height of 5 m under 2 m/s incident wind velocity.

6. EFFECT OF BUILDING HEIGHT ON RESULTING WIND VELOCITIES

It is well known that tall buildings in the built environment come with the advantage of wind resources in terms of high wind velocity [5] and the quality of flow is far better for energy generation, as revealed in Chapter 3, section 2.1.

In the following section, the effect of the height of a building alone on the resulting wind velocities due to the use of the above aerofoil shape is investigated. A number of building blocks of different heights were considered. The investigation is aimed at testing the aerofoil system for varying building heights regardless of the effect of altitude on wind velocity. A rectangular block 11 m wide and 22 m long is selected with the aerofoil running along its length. The chosen heights were 5, 10, 15 and 20 m, as shown in Fig. (**9**), Fig. (**10**), Fig. (**11**) and Fig. (**12**), respectively. The simulation employed a non-structural 3D grid with an asymmetry condition to its upper and side boundaries.

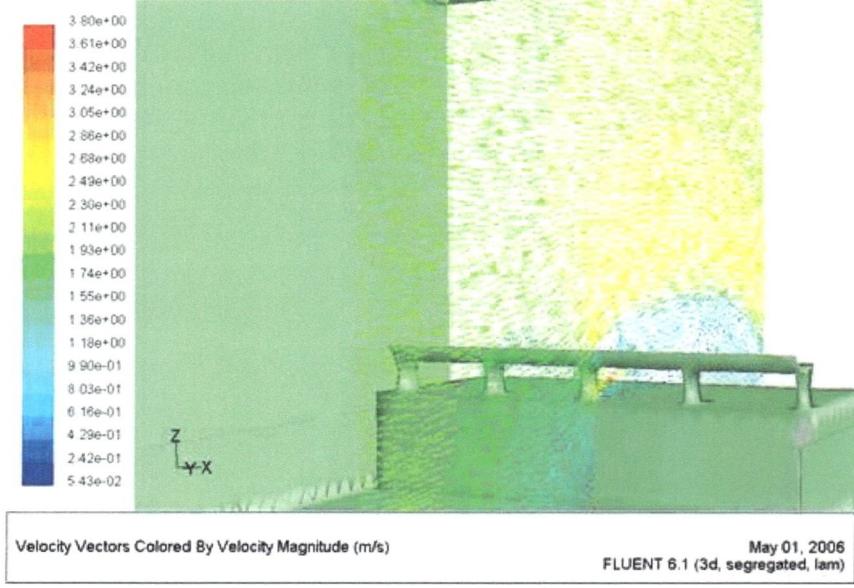

Fig. (10). Velocity vectors for building height of 10 m under 2 m/s incident wind velocity.

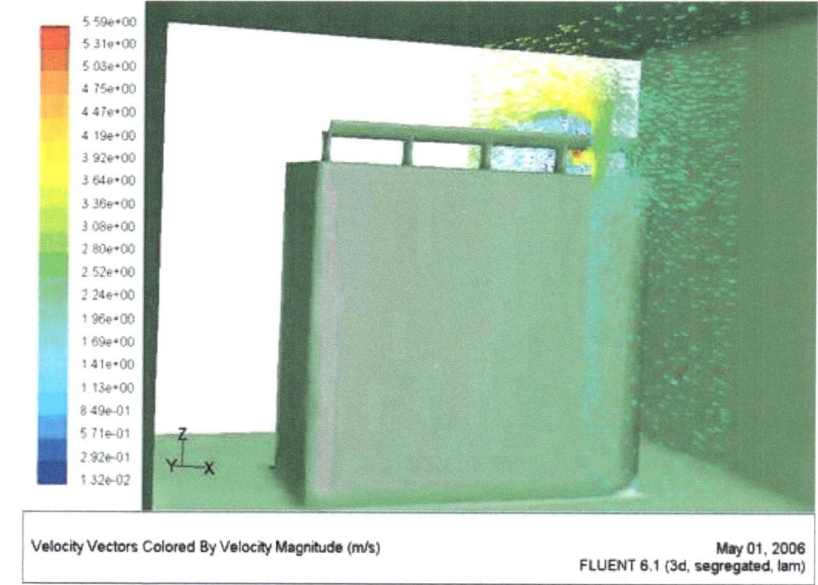

Fig. (11). Velocity vectors for building height of 15 m under 2 m/s incident wind velocity.

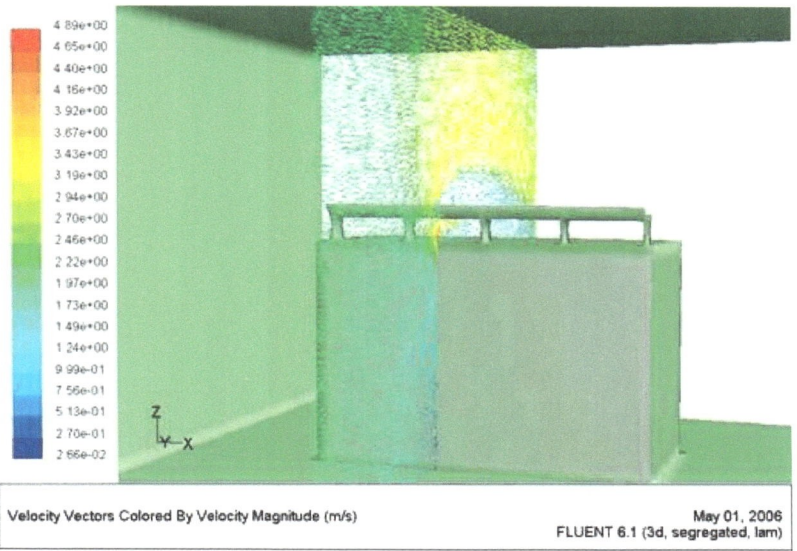

Fig. (12). Velocity vectors for building height of 20 m under 2 m/s incident wind velocity.

6.1. Results of the Effect of Building Height

The effect of the building height on the resulting wind velocities under the aerofoil for different incident wind velocities have been illustrated in Fig. (**13**) and Fig. (**14**).

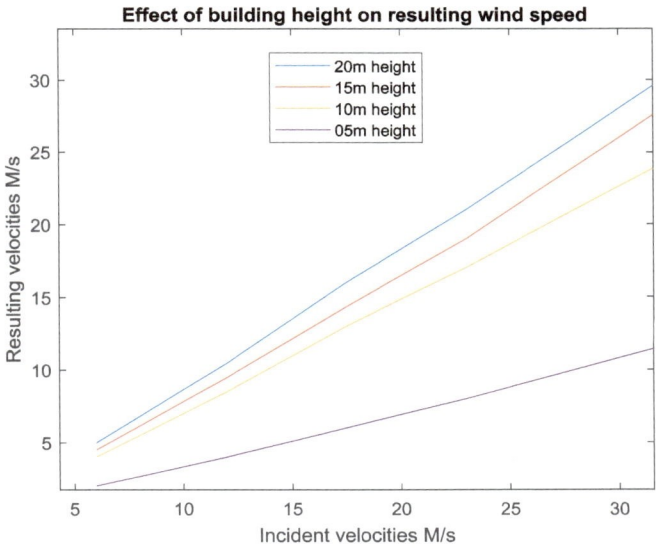

Fig. (13). Effect of building height on resulting wind velocities.

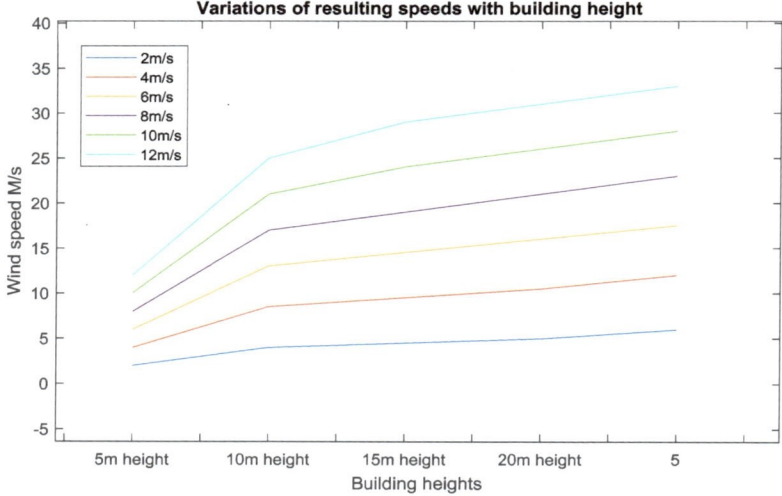

Fig. (14). Variations in resulting wind velocities with changes in the building height.

These figures show that with the increase in building height leads to an increase in the resulting wind velocities yielded by the aerofoil. This draws our attention to the fact that when the design of the aerofoil and all the other factors remain the same, taller buildings are likely to receive higher resulting wind velocities under the aerofoil than shorter buildings of the same dimensions.

CONCLUSION

- The optimisation of aerofoil parameters can enhance control over wind separation and eventually lead to both lower resistance to flow and better energy harvesting.

- Wind flow patterns under the aerofoil can vary from localised jets under the aerofoil to the entire area under the aerofoil flowing as a high-velocity jet of air. Optimisation generally leads to the entire area being under the influence of the highest wind velocity. However, localised jets may be preferably for Savonius wind turbines.

- The incorporation of turbines under the aerofoil eliminated flow separation on the leeward side.

- Wind acceleration under the aerofoil would be higher when no turbines are integrated. However, optimising aerofoil parameters ensures the highest possible wind acceleration under the aerofoil with turbine integration.

- Turbine resistance lowers the pressure drop.

- With an increase in incident wind velocities, the pressure drop across the turbines increases. However, optimisation of the aerofoil would accumulate the lowest possible pressure drop, which normally leads to higher power generation.

- Varying the turbine resistance (*i.e.* varying porosity percentage across the porous jump) for any particular wind velocity provides constant resulting wind velocities and pressure drops regardless of the variations in porosity.

- The optimised case produced from 650.8 to 823 W/m^2 of power depending on the incident wind velocities, while the unoptimised case generated from 400 to 438.4 W/m^2 of power for the same incident wind velocities.

- Optimising the aerofoil produced 1.6–1.9 times more energy than that produced by the unoptimised cases, while turbine positioning produced 3.38 times more energy than that of the optimised case with the turbine positioned near the rear of the aerofoil.

- The effect of geographical altitude and building height reinforces that tall buildings have high potential of securing the highest incident wind velocities and are therefore better for harvesting wind energy.

REFERENCES

[1] A.R. Elbakheit, "Effect of turbine resistance and positioning on performance of aerofoil wing building augmented wind energy generation", *Energy Build.*, vol. 174, pp. 365-371, 2018.
[http://dx.doi.org/10.1016/j.enbuild.2018.06.025]

[2] K. Rajendra, M.R.A. Pachauri, and J. Christ, "AR5 synthesis report: climate change 2014 — IPCC", In: *IPCC, Geneva, Switzerland, AB*, 2014, p. 151.

[3] A.R. Elbakheit, "Factors enhancing aerofoil wings for wind energy harnessing in buildings", *Build. Serv. Eng. Res. Tech.*, vol. 35, no. 4, pp. 417-437, 2014.
[http://dx.doi.org/10.1177/0143624413509097]

[4] S.J. Watson, D.G. Infield, J.P. Barton, and S.J. Wylie, "Modelling of the performance of a building - mounted ducted wind turbine", *J. Phys. Conf. Ser.*, vol. 75, p. 012001, 2007.
[http://dx.doi.org/10.1088/1742-6596/75/1/012001]

[5] S. Mertens, *Wind description for roof location of wind turbines, a design guideline or the required height of a wind turbine on a horizontal roof of a mid- to high-rise building.*, Proc Global Wind power Paris: France, 2002.

CHAPTER 7

Conclusion

When considering the architectural design process in general and system-based architectural design in particular, the architectural form-finding process can be further elaborated by taking wind energy generation potential on board. However, as usual, every building design has it peculiar set of requirements from the client's brief, code requirements, context site stipulations, just to name a few, which also must be accounted for. Therefore, each building design is unique and tailor-made. Aerodynamic architectural design follows suit in this regard. However, there are principles of air movements that should be considered as opportunities to arrive at good working solutions. In this sense, aerodynamic form may resemble the acoustical form in the careful planning, arrangements need to be in place, and then, testing/simulation and optimisation are done until a final resolution is obtained. Thus, the architectural design palette of form finding could be further enhanced with aerodynamic optimisations to achieve sustainability. Whereas the acoustical form represents favourable sound performance and interior views of auditoriums, aerodynamic form represents the visual image of the project, in addition to invisible, but quantifiable, valuable renewable energy. Thus, the entire architectural form of the project has to mix the architectural expressions with wind aerodynamics. Another benefit of aerodynamically optimised architectural forms is that it takes full control of the building's structural stability and eliminates vortex shedding through the choice of unsymmetrical, carefully sculpted forms. Not optimising architectural aerodynamic forms may render buildings susceptible to huge costs of employing structural damping measures and solutions. Tall buildings benefit from the high wind energy potential compared to low-rise buildings owing to their height and the unobstructed air flow of the upper atmospheric layers. Architectural form for wind energy generation capabilities can be optimised, gauged and compared based on 'capacity factor' determination, which provides an indication of how the design improves wind energy generation potential in a particular site, thereby gauging its level of sustainability.

This book proposes a number of aerodynamically stable forms of tall buildings along with measures for combating vortex shedding, of which, rotational forms are generally considered one of the safest forms that exhibit high stability in wind tunnel tests and CFD smulations. Moreover, architectural design may utilise natural wind movements as an impetus for both natural ventilation and wind energy generation.

Low-rise buildings lead to more of wind separation occurring at the corners of the built environment since they evoke wind acceleration amenable for harvesting using the right technology.

A simultaneous product of wind separation is a varied distribution of pressures, which leads to suctions, turbulences and uplifting. These may be resolved by the right forms of profiles of aerofoils as well as by the right choice of materials that may limit if not eliminate the unwanted effects of wind separation.

Otherwise, resolution to some special structural design has to be made. Structures have always been the backbones of architecture. Their role may extend to supporting some architectural designs integrated with wind energy generation equipment for stability. In addition, the Bernoulli effect, Venturi effect and stack effect are techniques to generate continuous fairly speedy streams of air that could be employed for building-integrated wind energy systems.

Aerofoils are an invaluable asset in streamlining wind separation around buildings, and the therefore assist wind turbines in receiving the laminar flow needed for successful operation. The acceleration between aerofoils and buildings occurs because for an incompressible fluid flow, the product of the flow velocity and cross-sectional area at any point along the flow within a restriction is constant. This can be expressed as follows:

$$V_1 A_1 = V_2 A_2 = V_n A_n, \qquad (3) \text{ (Chapter 2)}$$

where V is the flow velocity at a point and A is cross-sectional area at the same point.

Hence, the velocity V_2 can be increased to the desired value by reducing the area A_2 accordingly.

When considering quantifying the wind resources at a given site, wind energy availability can be obtained from accurately simulated data in addition to the metrological data. However, the former is not always readily accessible, while the latter is normally confined to macro levels. Nevertheless, each site has its own architectural form that entirely dictates the type of wind regime.

CFD assists in examining flow conditions around buildings and guide processes of optimising wind flows for optimum performance of wind energy generation technologies.

The study has confirmed the usefulness of aerofoils in augmenting wind flows that could be harvested using turbine's efficiencies exceeding the Betz limit compared to those of standalone turbines.

The investigated aerofoil profile could accelerate wind velocities by factors varying from 0.53 to 3.5 times compared to those under the Betz limit, *i.e.* from below the limit to over 6 times over the limit, depending on present wind flows.

Aerofoil profiles to boost wind energy generation can be incorporated into buildings during the design stage or after construction. Small- to medium-sized vertical-axis Savonious wind turbines are recommended for use with aerofoils.

The main factors influencing wind acceleration into turbines using aerofoils are the proximity of the aerofoil to the building surfaces and the angle of attack.

This investigation revealed that an angle of attack of 50° would assist aerofoils under consideration achieve the highest possible wind acceleration.

The proximity of aerofoil to the roof of the building that delivered the highest possible wind acceleration is 85 cm.

This investigation has shown that aerofoil position has a great influence on the ensuing wind acceleration. Aerofoil positioning together with careful planning for wind separations secures successful performance.

This process can be applied to any given building design situation to guarantee optimum performance.

Aerofoil parameter optimisation can enhance control over wind separation and can eventually lead to both lower resistances to flow and better energy harvesting.

Wind flow patterns under the aerofoil can vary from localised jets under the aerofoil to the entire area under the aerofoil flowing as a high-velocity jet of air. Optimisation generally leads to the entire area being under the influence of the highest wind velocity. However, localised jets may be much suited to Savonius wind turbines.

The incorporation of wind turbines under the aerofoil eliminated flow separation on the leeward side.

Wind acceleration under the aerofoil would be higher when no turbines are integrated. However, optimising aerofoil parameters ensures the highest possible wind acceleration under the aerofoil even after turbine integration.

Turbine resistance to flow lowers the pressure drop.

With the increase in incident wind velocities, the pressure drop across the turbines increases. However, the optimisation of the aerofoil would accumulate the lowest possible pressure drop, which normally leads to more power generation.

Varying turbine resistance (*i.e.* varying the porosity percentage across the porous jump) for any particular wind velocity, provides constant resulting wind velocity and pressure drop regardless of the porosity variations.

The turbine position under the aerofoil may dictate how well it may perform considering that both the resulting wind velocities and pressure drop are acting simultaneously on it. Towards the front of the aerofoil on the windward side, there is higher pressure, while towards the rear of the aerofoil there is higher wind velocity.

Optimising the aerofoil produced 1.6–1.9 times more energy than that produced by the unoptimised cases, while turbine positioning produced 3.38 times more than that of the optimised case from the rear of aerofoil position.

Regardless of the altitude, tall buildings are more susceptible to receive high wind velocities owing to their height. The taller they get, the more wind energy they may generate. Therefore, we can deduce that tall buildings have two factors assisting with obtaining high wind velocities: geographical altitude and building height. Another form of power augmentation to wind energy generation from wind turbines can be achieved by using diffusers of different designs, affording 2–3 times higher energy output than standalone turbines. However, simple diffuser designs can be easily implemented to many types of turbine designs and sizes. One of the lessons learnt from diffuser designs that could be translated to building designs is the importance of the area ratio (*i.e.* outlet area over inlet area) and length–diameter ratio (*i.e.* length over diameter). The larger these ratios, the larger the expected power augmentations of these wind turbines will be.

SUBJECT INDEX

A

Accelerated wind flows 37
Accelerating 2, 4, 89
   onshore wind velocity 4
   wind flow 2, 89
Acceleration 13, 27, 36, 52, 69, 84, 90, 106
   circumferential velocity 84
Aerodynamic 21, 24, 33, 34, 75, 105
   aerofoils 34
   behaviour 75
   design 24, 33
   excitation 75
   forces 21
   optimisations 105
Aerofoil(s) 24, 34, 35, 51, 53, 54, 57, 59, 62, 64, 65, 66, 69, 71, 76, 77, 88, 89, 92, 99, 100, 103, 104, 106, 107, 108
   angle 69
   design 77
   distance 65
   front shape 66
   optimisation 24
   parameter optimisation 103, 107
   positioning 107
   position on Top 62
   profiles 51, 53, 54, 76, 107
   proximity 51, 54, 65, 69
   system 100
Air 13, 30, 26, 27, 68, 76, 78, 80, 82, 84
   density 68, 78
   drag 24
   Inertia 30
   infiltration 13
   inlets 76
   intake 84
   stratification 26
   velocity 27, 68, 80, 82
Air flow 34, 78, 79, 80
   rate 34, 79
   velocity 78
Air movements 51, 56, 105
   projecting 51
Amalgamations 13
Angle 14, 34, 66, 67, 68, 70, 83, 84
   extra helical 14
Ansys fluent 89
Architect bill dunster 1
Architectural
   aerodynamic forms 105
Architectural design 1, 2, 3, 4, 5, 7, 10, 11, 13, 21, 22, 24, 25, 49, 51, 52, 73, 88, 89, 105, 106
   process 105
   solutions 1
   expressions 105
   forms 1, 3, 4, 5, 10, 11, 13, 21, 22, 24, 25, 51, 52, 88, 89
   ideas 1
   safety 10
   soundness 10
   stability 1
Augmented wind 51, 76
   energy system 51
   turbines profiles 76

B

Bahrain World Trade Center (BWTC) 3, 6
Bernoulli's equations 77
Blade 76, 81, 89
   clearance 81
   detachment 89
Blowing air 76
Boundary conditions 54, 56, 59, 61, 62
   atmospheric 59
   unified 61
Boundary layer 25, 26, 54, 58
   atmospheric 54
   natural atmospheric 25
Building(s) 2, 5, 6, 8, 10, 11, 12, 22, 24, 25, 26, 31, 33, 34, 35, 37, 40, 51, 52, 54, 59, 62, 81, 88, 89, 100, 101, 102, 103, 104, 106, 108

augmented wind energy systems 88
blocks 100
clusters 40
concentrating 2
façade 8, 11, 53
height 54, 100, 101, 102, 103, 104, 108
houses 5
industry 51
integrated wind energy systems 106
integration 52, 81
wind-induced vibration in 10, 11
Building's aerodynamic performance 13
Building design 24, 31, 52, 71, 73, 86, 89, 105, 107, 108
optimisation for potential wind energy collection 31
situation 107

C

CFD 22, 51, 52, 54, 67, 88, 105
ansys fluent 88
capability 51
simulations 22, 52, 54, 67
smulations 105
Chimney stacks 26
Computational 13, 51, 54, 56, 70, 75, 88, 106
domain inlet boundary 54
fluid dynamics (CFD) 13, 51, 56, 70, 75, 88, 106
Conceptual architectural design of kidney-shaped twin towers 2
Convection-related wind movements 54
Corner chamfer 13
Crossflex building 52

D

Diffuser
designs 73, 77, 86, 108
rings 82
Diffusers 73, 76, 77, 78, 79, 80, 81, 82, 83, 84, 85, 86
dynamic 85

flat 77
multi-slot 82
perpendicular 81
rotating 81, 85, 86
straight-walled 76
technology 76
Dimensions, geometrical 31
Direction 40, 43, 64
and frequency of wind occurrence 40, 43
wind flows, opposite 64
Direct wind flow, facing 31
Distance, aerofoil's 90
Distribution 35, 40, 41, 44, 45, 46, 47, 48
calculated wind 41, 44, 45, 46, 47
predicted flow 35
Duct-augmented wind turbines 88
Ducted 52, 76
system 52
windmill 76
Ducted wind turbine 52
claiming 52
prototypes 52
Dynamic 10, 11, 30
oscillations 10, 11
viscosity 30

E

Earthquakes 11
Earth's rotation 25
Effect of 59, 69, 89, 90, 91, 94, 96, 102
aerofoil angle of attack and aerofoil proximity 69
building height on resulting wind velocities 102
models of turbulence 59
turbine resistance 89, 90, 91, 94, 96
Einstein summation convention 57
Energy 1, 2, 5, 7, 39, 40, 49, 56, 75, 88, 100, 104, 105, 108
conservation equations 56
density 40
harvest 2, 75
mechanical 75

renewable 105
solar 7, 40
turbine's 5
turbulent kinetic 56
Energy generation 2, 6, 25, 34, 37, 52, 83, 86, 100
annual 6
enabled increasing wind 2
hinder wind 37
optimise wind 52
Energy harvesting 10, 24, 35, 103, 107
highest wind 10
successful wind 35

F

Façades 5, 6, 7, 10, 11, 53, 57
building's 10
curtain-wall 53
opposite 11
Fibonacci spiral ascending plan 11
Flower-shaped structure 1
Fluid(s) 30, 56, 57
density 56
dynamics 56
Fossil fuels 40

G

Gear boxes 7, 80
Global wind atlas 39, 40, 41, 44, 45, 46, 47
Grid convergence study 58

H

Hexagonal cells 58

I

Igra's diffuser 77
Improvement 14, 49, 70, 73, 90
consistent power 70

incremental power 70
Incident wind velocities 51, 54, 58, 60, 62, 63, 65, 67, 68, 94, 96, 100, 101, 102, 104, 108
consecutive 65, 67, 68
single 94
Incompressible fluid flow 35, 106
Incremental power stablises 96
Indoor air 27
Inlet 27, 58, 76
area ratio 76
opening 27
velocity 58
Intensified wind velocities 10

K

Kidney-shaped twin towers 2
Kinematic viscosity 57

L

Laminar flow 28, 29, 33, 37, 43, 106
Land 3
breeze 3
shore 3
Large turbines 2, 83
Leeward side 5, 6, 8, 10, 33, 57, 64, 92, 99, 103, 107
Length 25, 58, 59, 73, 77, 83, 86, 100, 108
increasing 83
non-dimensional perpendicular 58

M

Magnitudes 51, 57, 64, 65
air flow 57
Mathematical modelling 76
Measures 22, 105
mechanical damping 22
structural damping 105
Mechanical energy conversion 75
Mechanical floor 8
Mechanisms 25
air movement 25

passive cooling 25
Mesh 57, 58
   adaptations 58
   independent Solution 57
   refinement 57
   size guidelines 58
Metrological registration offices 40
Mitigate building oscillation 11
Models 13, 14, 52, 54, 56, 58, 59, 60, 62, 67, 78
   actuator disk 78
   theoretical 52
   turbulent 59
   virtual 56
   wind tunnel 13
Modifications 13, 14
   aerodynamic 14
Momentum theory 76, 77
Movement, vertical air 26
Multi-ejectors 81

N

Natural 8, 24, 26, 54, 85
   boundary layer 26
   convection 54
   light utilisation, optimal 8
   pressured air 85
   ventilation mechanisms 24
Natural wind 25, 4, 105
   movements 105
   passage 4
   pressure 25
Noise 4, 6, 73, 74, 75, 89
   airborne 75
   levels, reducing 89
   loudest 74
   reduction 74

O

Obstructing wind flow 89
Obstructive force 54
Optimisation wind flows 70

Optimised architectural 1, 49, 105
   design 49
   forms 1, 105

P

Plausible option 89
Porosity variations 108
Porous jump 88, 89, 90, 92, 94, 96, 104, 108
   boundary condition 89
   plane 92, 94
Power 40, 42, 79
   coefficient 79
   density 40, 42
Power augmentation 83, 85, 108
   of energy generation 86
Power generation 40, 62, 68, 70, 96, 108
   anticipated 62
   steady 96
Power generation 69, 70, 100
   estimation 70, 100
   outcome 69
Pressure coefficient distribution 94
Pressure drop 77, 84, 88, 89, 92, 94, 96, 104, 107, 108
   losses, reducing 84
   drop surface 89
   reduced 92
Pressures 10, 27, 36, 37, 56, 78, 79, 82, 92, 106
   lower 82
   static 27
Process 24, 49, 51, 71, 105, 107
   architectural form-finding 105

R

Renewable energy 1, 27, 88
   sources 1, 27, 88
   technologies 88
Renewable devices 74
Reynold's number 29
Reynolds stress model (RSM) 54, 56, 59, 60, 61, 62, 63, 64, 67

Rhythmic excitation 74
Richardson extrapolation for grids 59
Roaches' grid convergence 58

S

Savonius wind turbines 92, 103, 107
Separation 11, 31, 58, 62, 79, 90
  produced double 62
  pronounced 90
Silent wind turbines 73
Solar 25, 27, 40, 48, 88
  chimneys 27
  harvesting technologies 48
  radiation heating 25
Solar energy 42, 48
  harvesting 42
  production 48
Sound waves 74
Source 1, 24, 39, 75, 76
  sustainable energy 24
Stability, structural 14, 21, 82, 105
Stack
  effect 26, 27, 28, 37, 106
  ventilation 26
Standalone wind turbine output 76
Streamlining 24, 34, 35, 36, 37, 80, 106
  wind separation 37, 106
Swift wind turbines 74
System-based architectural design 105

T

Tacoma narrows bridge 11
Tall buildings 7, 9, 10, 11, 13, 22, 26, 100, 104, 105, 108
  benefit 105
Technology 37, 51, 56, 84
  computational 56
  conversion 51
  multi-stage ejector 84
Tower 2, 4, 5, 6, 9, 27
  large kidney-shaped 2
  multiple 6

  twin 4
Turbine(s) 4, 5, 6, 9, 10, 39, 49, 51, 52, 53, 58, 73, 74, 75, 78, 79, 80, 83, 84, 85, 86, 88, 89, 92, 96, 99, 104, 107, 108
  blade 75
  designs 86, 108
  drag 85
  energy outcome 5
  five-bladed 6
  integration 104, 107
  lift type 89
  mechanical 39
  mixer ejector 84
  mounted 51, 52
  positions 9, 79, 99, 108
  shrouded 58
  small-scale 74
Turbine resistance 88, 89, 90, 91, 92, 93, 94, 95, 96, 97, 99, 101, 103, 104, 107, 108
  systematic architectural design 89, 91, 93, 95, 97, 99, 101, 103
Turbulence 31, 33, 34, 36, 37, 43, 53, 59, 62, 63, 64, 67, 77, 89
  high-intensity 67
  models 59, 63
  wake 77
Turbulent 28, 29, 30
  flow 29, 30
Twin towers taper skywards 4

V

Velocity 11, 12, 56
  component 56
  contours 11, 12
Velocity vectors 57, 63, 100, 101, 102
  for building height 100, 101, 102
Ventilation 1, 13, 24, 25, 26, 37, 105
  mix stack 26
  natural 24, 25, 37, 105
Ventilation 27, 28
  rate 27
  tower 28
Vernacular design 52

Vertical-axis wind turbines 52, 53, 71, 80, 81, 92
Vibrations 4, 11, 13, 53, 73, 75, 76, 85
  heavy 4
  high-frequency 75
  low-frequency 75
Vortex 1, 4, 9, 11, 14, 22, 75, 82, 83, 105
  pronounced 22
Vortex formation 82, 83
Vorticity-based diffusers 84

W

Walls 53, 58, 84
  bounding 58
  curved curtain 53
Water, running 36
Wind 2, 6, 8, 13, 24, 25, 27, 31, 39, 40, 49, 64, 65, 71, 75, 81, 82, 89, 100, 103, 104, 105, 106, 107
  acceleration 25, 71, 103, 104, 106, 107
  aerodynamic responses 24
  channel 89
  directions 40, 64, 65
  facing direct 31
  harvesting 6
  harvesting technologies 40
  high-velocity 75
  lens 82
  pressure 8, 13
  profiles 39
  resources 39, 49, 81, 100, 106
  tunnel tests 105
Wind energy 1, 3, 5, 39, 40, 48, 49, 51, 70, 71, 108
  industry 51
  integration 3, 51
  production 48
  resource 39
  technologies 51, 70
  variability 49
Wind energy harvesting 1, 2, 3, 6, 7, 8, 24, 31, 39, 42, 51, 104
  systems 6
  technologies 7
Wind energy generation 24, 25, 26, 33, 34, 36, 37, 39, 40, 49, 51, 52, 89, 105, 106, 107, 108
  capabilities 105
  complements 89
  enhancement 39
  equipment 106
  technologies 106
Wind flow(s) 2, 4, 6, 9, 11, 24, 25, 28, 31, 39, 43, 51, 53, 54, 71, 106
  augmenting 71, 106
  streamlining 62
  types 24
Wind forces 1, 5, 54
  excessive 1
Wind-induced vibrations 11, 13, 14, 75
  in wind turbines 75
Wind power 68, 85, 96
  equation 96
  resources 85
Wind turbine(s) 4, 5, 8, 10, 51, 52, 53, 68, 73, 74, 75, 76, 77, 78, 80, 86, 108
  augmented 73, 80
  designs 68
  industry 73
  integration 52, 53
  positions 10
Wind velocities 1, 4, 5, 6, 10, 11, 12, 13, 25, 26, 39, 40, 42, 43, 48, 51, 68, 69, 70, 71, 73, 74, 76, 89, 100, 108
  high 1, 6, 10, 13, 25, 39, 48, 51, 76, 100, 108
  low 26, 48, 51, 89
  triggering 10

www.ingramcontent.com/pod-product-compliance
Lightning Source LLC
Chambersburg PA
CBHW041831300426
44111CB00002B/55